KICK-START
Kindergarten Readiness

52 REPRODUCIBLE PARENT LETTERS!

- Social-emotional skills
- Math explorations
- Science inquiry
- Emerging literacy skills
- Language and vocabulary development
- Gross and fine motor skills

Alison Pepper

COPYRIGHT

Library of Congress Cataloging-in-Publication Data
The cataloging-in-publication data is registered with the Library of Congress for ISBN 978-0-87659-735-4.

Bulk Purchase

Gryphon House books are available for special premiums and sales promotions as well as for fund-raising use. Special editions or book excerpts also can be created to specifications. For details, call 800.638.0928.

Disclaimer

Gryphon House, Inc., cannot be held responsible for damage, mishap, or injury incurred during the use of or because of activities in this book. Appropriate and reasonable caution and adult supervision of children involved in activities and corresponding to the age and capability of each child involved are recommended at all times. Do not leave children unattended at any time. Observe safety and caution at all times.

TABLE OF CONTENTS

Introduction and How to Use This Book v

Chapter 1: Skills and Knowledge to Help Children Get Ready for Kindergarten 1

Chapter 2: Oral Language and Vocabulary 5

Chapter 3: Emerging Literacy 23

Chapter 4: Social-Emotional Skills 43

Chapter 5: Math Explorations 63

Chapter 6: Science Explorations 83

Chapter 7: Fine and Gross Motor Skills 101

References and Resources 120

Index 125

Gryphon House
www.gryphonhouse.com

INTRODUCTION AND HOW TO USE THIS BOOK

As teachers of four-year-old children, one of your primary considerations is how to best prepare the children in your classroom for their transition to kindergarten. Your school, your director, and local and federal licensing agencies all place a variety of requirements on you, so the activities and projects that you plan advance this readiness goal every day. Frequently, you may hear questions from families about how to best prepare their children for the next step into kindergarten. The pressure for the children's success may feel like it rests on your shoulders, but you don't have to do it alone. You have excellent allies—the children's families! Families are your partners in their children's education. In fact, they are their children's first teachers. Honoring that fact is empowering and will help you build an effective home-school connection.

This book is a tool to facilitate your efforts in engaging families and establishing the home-school connection. We know how busy you are! We offer you a variety of developmentally appropriate learning activities that you can send home to families each week so they can participate in their child's learning and can reinforce concepts and skills you are introducing in school. Each activity has been designed to help adults at home spend time on a specific play-based activity with their children. Learning comes naturally to children—they are curious, notice detail, and love to ask questions. Each activity gives families ways to support that innate curiosity.

How to Use This Book

What do children need to be ready to learn in kindergarten? Each week, choose a letter and accompanying activity to send home to families that will support learning in the following areas:

- Oral language and vocabulary

- Emerging literacy

- Social-emotional skills

- Math explorations

- Science investigations

- Fine and gross-motor skills

You can photocopy the letters and activities to send home with the children, or you can attach them to weekly emails or newsletters to families.

Each letter explains the learning that is taking place and offers a short note about the research behind why the activity supports that learning. The activities themselves are simple to do and require just a few commonly found materials—or no materials at all. Simple, specific instructions guide families in engaging their children in developmentally appropriate ways.

As families engage with their children at home, they can feel that they are directly contributing to their children's learning and future academic success. They can support the development of their children's independence and autonomy, emergent literacy, and cognitive and social-emotional skills and can advance children's understanding of the world around them. By participating in their children's learning using these guided activities, families will help prepare their children for an easy transition to kindergarten.

Gryphon House
www.gryphonhouse.com

CHAPTER 1

Skills and Knowledge to Help Children Get Ready for Kindergarten

Oral Language and Vocabulary

The ability to fully express themselves verbally is an important skill for kindergarten children. They need to communicate with peers to ask to play, to negotiate play, and to develop social relationships. They need to be able to tell an adult when they are upset or hurt or sick. They need to be able to express needs, such as hunger or needing to go to the bathroom. When young children can communicate needs, wants, and thoughts to adults and peers, they are able to feel more comfortable in the classroom setting and to open up whole worlds of learning in that environment.

Encourage family members to talk with and listen to their children. By simply naming objects and answering their children's questions as best they can, they will encourage important vocabulary growth. They can narrate household activities and chores. They can talk about objects and features they notice in the home and in the environment. They can sing songs and tell stories—especially those that reflect the family's culture. They can ask their children questions in a lighthearted way that encourages children to express their ideas and opinions. Simple encouragement and reinforcement at home will nurture children's oral language skills and vocabulary development to help them be ready for kindergarten.

Emerging Literacy

Four-year-old children are beginning to make the connection between spoken language and written symbols. While the typical preschooler is not quite reading yet, many are beginning to learn the names for some letters and the sounds that go with certain letters. They are also beginning to recognize print that they commonly see in the environment. Families can support this natural curiosity about letters and writing with simple activities at home. One of the best ways to support emerging literacy is to simply read to the child. Encourage families to read to their children every day. Invite them to check out books from the local library, and consider letting children take home books from the classroom book center to read with their families. Families can support letter recognition by encouraging their children to look for letters and words both at home and in the environment. They can sing, make up silly rhymes to play with letter sounds, and encourage their children to write letters and words.

Social-Emotional Skills

Social-emotional skills are so important to a child's success in kindergarten. Young children are just learning how to interact with others, how to wait for a turn, how to ask to play with a friend, and how to handle and express their emotions. They do not need to be experts in all of these skills by the time they start kindergarten, but they are certainly beginning to learn them.

Families can support their children's social-emotional learning through simple activities at home. They can help children name emotions: "I see you frowning. I think you might be mad," or "I see you smiling. Are you happy?" They can help their children learn to problem solve: "Let's see. You both want the truck. What can you do so both of you get a turn with it?" Encourage families to reinforce social-emotional awareness at home with activities such as playing games and doing puzzles together, taking turns in a family dance party, and finding ways for their child to be a helper at home.

Math Explorations

Math is a natural part of children's play. They decide how many plates and cups they need for their restaurant in the dramatic play center. They learn to connect number words, such as *one* and *two*, with the quantities those words represent. They learn to connect shape names with the shapes they represent. As they play board games, they learn to count the number of spaces to move their tokens without counting a space twice or skipping a space. Math appears in children's songs and books— "How many pigs? One, two, three!" Young children love to help. Math is part of sorting laundry by color or type of clothing.

Encourage families to support their children's math learning with simple, fun activities to share at home. As children become more familiar with vocabulary around numbers and shapes, they will be more confident in their math explorations.

Science Explorations

Children are natural scientists. They love to ask questions: How does a seed grow? Why are some leaves yellow? What will happen if I put water in the freezer? How many blocks tall am I? What does a cat (or gerbil or turtle) need to grow and be healthy? Instead of simply answering their children's questions, encourage families to explore these questions and let the children make scientific discoveries about the world around them. Through observing, wondering, questioning, predicting, experimenting, and thinking, children develop critical-thinking skills that will lay the foundations for more science learning in kindergarten.

Fine and Gross Motor Skills

Preschool children are growing quickly and learning to use their bodies as they become stronger and more agile. This is the perfect time to support their explorations and newfound skills to help them get ready for kindergarten. Young children are experimenting with gross-motor skills as they balance, jump, run, catch, throw, kick, and climb. Their fine-motor skills improve when they have opportunities to use their forefingers and thumbs in pincer movements and lacing activities and to use their whole hands to smush and mold playdough, explore sand, or paint with fingerpaints.

Encourage families to engage their children in the fun activities included in this book. They can explore throwing a small ball overhand and underhand, tossing a bean bag or kicking a ball at a target, jumping and hopping as they play hopscotch, balancing on one foot and on a low beam, and climbing on playground equipment. Families can enjoy exploring the textures of and sculpting with homemade playdough, painting with tools and with fingers (and toes!), using child-safe scissors to cut paper, lacing yarn or ribbon through cardboard, and sifting objects from sand.

With confidence in their abilities, the children will feel ready to meet the exciting challenges of kindergarten!

Gryphon House
www.gryphonhouse.com

CHAPTER **2**

Oral Language and Vocabulary

Dear families:

Words, words, words—everywhere we go, we see words! Children are exposed to lots of different kinds of print in books, newspapers, magazines, on signs, and on the street.

Help your child enrich his or her vocabulary by paying attention to the words in your surroundings. As you walk in your neighborhood or go about your daily business, help your child notice signs, logos, and symbols. Read the signs to your child and talk about what they mean. Point out a letter and make that letter sound.

At home, you can create a print-rich environment for your child by placing labels on objects, such as a chair, a window, and the refrigerator. Point out the labels to your child and read them aloud. Although you shouldn't expect your child to read at this stage, this simple activity will help your child learn to recognize new words, recognize letters, and understand the purpose of printed language—to communicate! Developing this understanding of print will build a foundation as your child begins to understand that words have meaning.

Sincerely,

Your child's teacher

Gryphon House
www.gryphonhouse.com

LABELING AT HOME

What I Need

Magic marker
Thick paper, oak tag, or a file folder
Masking tape or painter's tape
Scissors (adult use only)

What to Do

1. Ahead of time, cut a bunch of 4- to 5-inch rectangle cards that you can use for your labels.

2. Start in the kitchen, and ask your child to help you in a labeling game. Your child will be very familiar with labeling, as we do it our classroom.

3. Ask your child what appliances and items to label. Choose between five and seven items.

4. One at a time, write the word for each item on a card. Say the letters aloud as you write them: "W-I-N-D-O-W. *Window* starts with *W. W* makes the /w/ /w/ sound."

5. Ask your child to tape the label on the object. Try to keep the labels at your child's eye level wherever possible. Read the labels aloud.

6. Return to review the labels with your child in a couple of days. Add a few more labels if you wish.

7. Leave the labels up as long as you feel comfortable having them around.

What My Child Is Learning

As you expose your child to labels, he or she is learning to make connections between the object and the word name. Your child's vocabulary increases as a result, and this will support his or her emerging ability to recognize some letters and, later, begin to read.

What the Research Says

Researchers have found that exposure to written language helps children develop an awareness of print, letter naming, and phonemic awareness. Through exposure to oral language, preschool children develop listening comprehension, vocabulary, and language skills.

Dear families:

Wherever we go, we see words popping out at us—on the street as we walk, drive, or ride; as we shop; and as we relax at home. Many words we see over and over again on street signs, store names, traffic signs, subway posters, newspaper stands, and so on. As children start to notice letters and words, they begin to recognize the "picture" of a common word. Most often that starts with the child's name. Then they start to notice logos and symbols that are prominent in the community. That's emergent literacy—that's beginning to read!

Finding words everywhere is exciting for children, especially when you join in the game with them. This is a great way to make early reading fun!

Sincerely,

Your child's teacher

ON THE STREET—FINDING WORDS EVERYWHERE

What I Need

No materials needed

What to Do

1. Go for a walk or a ride with your child.

2. As you go, talk with your child. Read signs that you see. Pay attention to the words that catch your child's eye.

3. Point out letters that your child may recognize. "Look! That stop sign has the letter *S*. Your name starts with *S*."

4. Make a game of finding words everywhere. How many stop signs can your child find? What does that sign tell us about that shop? What is that poster advertising?

5. Draw attention to words all around to help accelerate your child's understanding of the importance of language in both speaking and reading. Your child will gain confidence and joy in the ability to recognize letters and words, and that will ultimately lead to a love of reading!

What My Child Is Learning

Recognizing letters, logos, and words are some of the early stages in learning to read.

What the Research Says

Researchers have found that exposure to written language helps children develop an awareness of print, letter naming, and phonemic awareness. Through exposure to oral language, preschool children develop listening comprehension, vocabulary, and language skills.

Dear families:

One of our objectives in preparing your children for kindergarten is to build their vocabulary and comprehension of more words to develop their oral language skills.

Every single day you can introduce new vocabulary to your child as you speak with him or her about everyday life. Don't be afraid to use "big" words—children love them. Consider, for example, how young children seem to know the names of every dinosaur! As their vocabulary increases, so will their confidence and ability to express themselves clearly.

For this week's activity, we will play a simple and easy word game: I Spy. Be playful and think of amusing ways to play with your child.

Sincerely,

Your child's teacher

Gryphon House
www.gryphonhouse.com

I SPY

What I Need

No materials needed

What to Do

1. With your child, as you ride around town doing errands, head out on a family trip, or simply relax at home, look for interesting items or people in the environment. These could be a billboard, a large tree, a building, the refrigerator, a person in a brightly colored outfit, a person walking a dog—almost anything will work.

2. Notice something in the immediate environment. Then begin the game by saying, "I spy with my little eye something . . ." and fill in an adjective. For example, if you see a traffic cone, you could say, "I spy with my little eye something orange."

3. Your child can then look around and offer a guess about what you are referring to. If your child becomes frustrated, you can offer more hints, such as "I spy something orange and cone shaped."

4. When the child guesses correctly, he or she becomes the leader for the next round.

What My Child Is Learning

This game encourages your child to develop observation skills and notice details of objects in the world around them. Your child will build vocabulary and oral language as he or she thinks of words to describe what he or she is seeing or listens to the descriptions you offer. Your child will use logic and reasoning to draw conclusions about what you are describing.

What the Research Says

Engaging children in rich conversations about interesting content supports vocabulary development.

Dear families:

Invite your child to join in with you as you do housework! While it might take you a bit longer to compete some of the tasks, it's a great way to spend time together. As you do simple household tasks, your child will increase his or her vocabulary, learn to follow directions, and increase his or her fine and gross-motor skills.

What could you do together? How about wash dishes, sort and fold laundry, sweep the floor, or pick up and put away toys? As you work, narrate everything that you do so your child understands the steps and learns the correct words to describe the activity. Consider what household chores you can do together easily, and get going!

Sincerely,

Your child's teacher

DOING HOUSEHOLD CHORES TOGETHER

What I Need

Materials will vary, depending on the task

What to Do

1. Think of some household tasks in which you can cooperatively engage your child. Consider, for example, sweeping the kitchen floor. You and your child can discover rich vocabulary in this simple activity.

2. Ask your child to help you. Show him or her how to hold the broom and how to move it across the floor to gather up the dirt.

3. As you work together, talk about what you are doing. For example, use position words such as *under*, *behind*, and *over*: "Dirt likes to hide under this rug. Let's sweep under there." "I see some dust bunnies behind this chair. Can you sweep behind the chair?" "We've tracked in a lot of dirt this week. Let's sweep over the floor in the kitchen to get it all up."

4. Be sure to compliment your child on working so hard and helping out around the house.

What My Child Is Learning

With every chore, there are vocabulary words to learn, steps to accomplish the task, and attention to detail. With even the smallest task, your child will learn to work cooperatively. Encourage your child to talk about what you are doing, and have conversations about not only the task but also why it is necessary. Your child will gain increased self-esteem as he or she learns that he or she is a capable and helpful member of the family.

What the Research Says

Multiple studies support the idea that children learn vocabulary in social contexts and interaction with others. Through exposure to oral language, children develop listening comprehension, vocabulary, and language skills.

Dear families:

Plan a visit to a local museum with your child. Ahead of time, take a look at the museum website, and decide together what you want to see on this visit. Focus on the subject matter and the vocabulary that is unique to the exhibit and the museum. Exploring in this way will increase your child's understanding of new words and expand his or her oral language.

Make the visit entertaining by searching for things in categories. For example, find five objects made of metal, look for items that are a certain color, or find paintings with animals in them. This will keep your child's interest and make your visit fun.

Of course, before you head to the museum, talk with your child about how to behave there. Be considerate of the other visitors, don't run and shout, and only touch exhibits if the museum allows this. Enjoy your outing!

Sincerely,

Your child's teacher

MUSEUM VISIT

What I Need

Online access

What to Do

1. Look for a museum in your area. Go online to the museum's website to learn what exhibits it offers. If you are not sure what is available in your area, talk with your child's teacher or a librarian to get ideas.

2. With your child, choose an exhibit to visit. Explore the museum's website with your child, discussing what you may see at the museum. For example, if you plan on visiting an art exhibit, talk about the paintings, sculptures, or other art you will see.

3. Remind your child about the museum's rules, such as no climbing on a sculpture or no touching the art (unless the museum allows it—some do).

4. Visit one exhibit, and use vocabulary that is specific to the exhibit. Read the signs hanging by the art pieces or look at a museum brochure to help you know what to point out to your child: "This artist grew up in Argentina. Wow, that's really far away. He uses chalk to make his pictures. Hey! We could make pictures with chalk, too!"

5. Search for things in categories. For example, look for five objects made of metal, items that are a certain color, or paintings with animals in them.

6. When you return home, ask your child if he or she would like to draw or sculpt some of the things seen at the museum. Give your child drawing materials or playdough, and discuss the work together afterward, writing down some of the things he or she says.

What My Child Is Learning

In museums, children are exposed to new cultures, history, ways of living, and art that broadens their horizons. Exposure to new subjects and environments encourages your child to learn new vocabulary. Learning new words increases your child's ability to express him- or herself in more detail.

What the Research Says

Authors Kevin Crowley and Melanie Jacobs point out that museum visits are valuable experiences for young children. "Young children delight in being in the presence of 'the real thing.'. . . [They] make personal connections to what they see in the museum, and they respond especially well when stories and the use of their imaginations are part of the experience."

Dear families:

Many people have favorite songs that they love to listen to. Often these songs may reflect a person's culture and country of birth. Playing or singing the sounds and rhythms you love creates an incredible opportunity to share your family's heritage with your child. So often, we hear musicians speak about the music they heard as children as being a main influence in their creativity and musical paths.

Sing your favorite songs or play music you love to introduce your child to the tunes. He or she will learn to appreciate music and perhaps be influenced to explore more music on his or her own. It's an easy way to explore family history and culture plus learn wonderful melodies rich in new vocabulary. Whether the songs are in English or your native language, your child will pick up the lyrics and melody and will learn a new way to express him- or herself.

Sincerely,

Your child's teacher

SINGING FAMILY SONGS TOGETHER

What I Need

A few favorite songs to sing to your child
Recordings of favorite songs (optional)

What to Do

1. Play music at home and when you travel to expose your child to different kinds of music and songs. Sing your favorite songs, and invite your child to join in with you.

2. Talk with your child about why you love a particular song. If it connects to your family heritage, explain that connection to your child.

3. If possible, let your child have access to his or her own musical selections over time.

4. Sing together and share music whenever possible.

What My Child Is Learning

Playing or singing the sounds and rhythms you love is an opportunity to teach your child your family's heritage. Music teaches new vocabulary from the songs' lyrics and an understanding of rhythm and tempo, and it supports memory activation as you recall the lyrics and music as you sing together.

What the Research Says

Researcher Elizabeth Carlton asserts that "music experiences . . . can make many valuable connections to our children's language capabilities, memory, physical activity, creative thinking, emotional stability, discipline, and emerging academic success. As brain research begins to support the importance of learning through music, we must continue to find useful ways to make the gifts music provides essential in our daily routine."

Dear families:

We want children to feel comfortable and secure in their home environment and community. Learning about their surroundings, the people who live there, and the community's uniqueness is an excellent way to build your child's vocabulary and language fluency while introducing him or her to the area you live in.

Strive to develop your child's confidence and familiarity with your neighborhood. Asking and answering questions about the world right outside your door is important for your child's development.

Sincerely,

Your child's teacher

Gryphon House
www.gryphonhouse.com

LET'S LEARN ABOUT OUR NEIGHBORHOOD

What I Need

No materials needed

What to Do

1. Whenever you're out for a walk or a ride in your neighborhood with your child, invite him or her to ask questions about what he or she notices. See what catches your child's interest.

2. Talk about where you live. Is it a big city? a small town? a quiet country place? What are the elements that are unique to the place?

3. Talk about the kind of transportation you use. What other choices are available in your area? Point out buses, trains, or other types of transportation that people use.

4. Talk about your neighbors, their families, and what they do. Do they have children or pets? How many family members do they have?

5. Extend these conversations according to your child's interests.

What My Child Is Learning

By engaging your child in conversation about your neighborhood, you will be helping him or her develop new vocabulary as he or she explores and identifies new things. Your young one will develop self-confidence, which will encourage him or her to continue to observe and explore wherever he or she may travel. Your child will grow in familiarity with your community and what makes it unique.

What the Research Says

Author Jeanne Vergeront says that understanding place is an important way in which we make meaning of the world. Fundamentally, place is where we come from, where we feel alive, and where we find the past in the present moment. We want to know and be where we are. We share places with others, return to places that hold meaning, and remember and tell stories brimming with place.

Dear families:

Young children love to learn rhyming poems and enjoy the story and humor found in them. Rhyme, rhythm, and repetition are incredibly important for small children. They feel competent when they learn a new rhyme and proud when they master the words.

The rhythms and rhymes of poems and songs help children move from spoken language to written language. As children explore and enjoy nursery rhymes, they expand their vocabulary and oral language. Choose a few nursery rhymes that you knew as a child, or find a book of rhymes at the library and discover a few new favorites to share.

Sincerely,

You child's teacher

LEARNING NURSERY RHYMES

What I Need

Nursery rhymes, either ones you know or some from a book

What to Do

1. Read or recite nursery rhymes to your child. You can do this when you're riding in a car or on a bus, when you're going for a walk, at bath time or bedtime, or anytime you have a few minutes.

2. Repeat them as many times as your child enjoys them. Repetition allows children to become familiar with and memorize the rhymes and to join in the fun.

What My Child Is Learning

Rhyme, rhythm, and repetition are all elements of oral language development. Understanding these elements is a starting point for learning to read.

What the Research Says

Beloved children's author Mem Fox says, "I know that if children cannot learn the skill of predicting what's going to come next in language, they can't learn to read. They have to know what's coming next in a sentence. . . . The ability to predict language is crucial to learning to read."

CHAPTER 3

Emerging Literacy

Dear families:

Children love to listen to adults tell stories. Whether the stories are true or fiction, children just adore lying back and listening as they let their imaginations "see" the tale. We have so few opportunities today for our children to listen to stories that aren't in books or on TV. It takes a special kind of attention and a quiet spot, such as bedtime, to effectively tell and listen to a story.

You can develop your child's oral language through storytelling. Use your imagination, and adjust your stories to fit your family's traditions and culture. Think about a unique family story, retell a familiar favorite children's story, or just make one up on the spot! Simply hearing your voice telling a tale will enchant your child. Guaranteed, your child will be attentive and love every second!

Sincerely,

Your child's teacher

ORAL STORYTELLING

What I Need

- An oral story no longer than five to seven minutes
- A quiet spot and time

What to Do

1. Find a quiet time and place to share the story. Bedtime is a great time for storytelling.

2. Tell your story. As you do, use different voices for the different characters, and don't forget to make animated faces as you talk! Your child will watch for facial expressions and listen to voice tones for clues about the characters in the story.

3. Answer your child's questions: "How big was the giant? He was sooooo big! Bigger than this apartment building!"

4. Tell the story again and again if your child is interested.

5. Have fun with the story and embellish it if you can. Add a new character or change the setting; for example, if the story takes place in a forest, change it to take place at the beach or in a city.

6. Invite your child to retell the story in his or her own words. Encourage your child to act it out or to illustrate the story in drawings.

7. Invite your child to create his or her own story and tell it to you.

What My Child Is Learning

Language develops long before a child speaks actual words. Since there is a natural progression of oral language to reading and writing, telling stories is an important step to becoming a reader. Your child will learn to listen carefully to keep up with the story line and use his or her imagination to follow the story.

What the Research Says

Researcher Jackie Peck found that a story told aloud can be an exciting and meaningful personal experience for young children, one that provides the incentive to retell and create stories for themselves. Author Jack Maguire asserts that storytelling also increases concentration and the ability to think symbolically and metaphorically.

Dear families:

One of the easy activities you can do with your child is to read storybooks aloud. Children adore listening to stories, and with a good selection of books from your local library, bookstore, or our classroom library, you can enjoy quality time with your child.

I can provide you with a list of age-appropriate books. Children love to hear stories over and over again and then "read" them on their own, so having some age-appropriate books in your home is recommended.

One of the greatest pleasures in life is reading—it opens up whole new worlds. Encouraging your child to love reading is a powerful and long-lasting gift.

Sincerely,

Your child's teacher

READ BOOKS ALOUD TO YOUR CHILD

What I Need

Age-appropriate books

What to Do

1. Establish a regular story time. This may be after dinner, at bedtime, or at another time that works with your family's schedule.

2. Choose a book or two with your child, and snuggle up so you both can see the pictures and words.

3. Read the story. As you read, point to the words so your child can follow along.

4. Spend time on each page. Look at, point to, and discuss the illustrations or photos with your child: "I see a red frog! Do you see it? Do you see any other animals?"

5. Answer any questions your child may have or extend his or her comments with more information or questions: "Yes, that's a lion. What sound does a lion make? Do you see the lion's legs? Let's count them: one, two, three, four."

6. Talk together about the story when you have finished reading the book.

7. Allow your child to physically explore books by making them easily accessible after you've read them together. Remind your child about caring for and being gentle with books—something we have learned in school. Encourage your child to turn pages and pretend to read on his or her own and retell the story in his or her own words.

What My Child Is Learning

Your child's vocabulary increases as he or she hears new words in books. Reading exposes him or her to subtle variations in word meanings. Your child will develop emergent literacy skills by showing an interest in books. Imitating the behavior of reading will allow your child to explore and begin to grasp the overall concept of reading. He or she will soon begin to develop an awareness of words and pictures.

What the Research Says

Researchers have found that storybook reading at home is an important part of giving children contact with written materials to support their emerging reading skills.

Dear families:

In our community, there are public libraries available for you and your child to use freely. Visiting the library is a wonderful opportunity to spend quiet time with each other, to choose special books to bring home to read aloud together, and to help prepare your child for kindergarten.

While we have a library at school, the public library has so many more books to select from, and the librarians are always helpful when you are looking for a special topic or book. Many public libraries offer story times for children of different ages. Inquire when there will be story hour readings for your child's age group. Find a special day and time you can go to the library with your child—perhaps once a week. Your whole family will enjoy it!

Sincerely,

Your child's teacher

FAMILY LIBRARY VISIT

What I Need

Find your local library

What to Do

1. Plan a time to visit your local public library. If you don't already have one, sign up for a library card. The librarian will be happy to help you with this. Often, children can get their own card if they can write their full name.

2. Decide with your child how many books you will check out. "You can choose five books to take home, and we can read two books while we are here."

3. Limit the visit to thirty to forty-five minutes. Remind your child to be quiet and speak in a whisper so you don't disturb other people who are visiting the library.

4. Find the section where there are books appropriate for your child's age, and browse together.

5. Ask for the librarian's assistance if you are looking for a special book or topic. One search might be to find children's books about a child transitioning from pre-K to kindergarten. Reading books that reflect your child's experience help him or her gain confidence and know that his or her concerns are also reflected in the stories you are reading.

6. Choose the specific number of books to take home that you and your child have agreed on, and check them out.

7. Have a special time at home to read aloud to your child every day.

What My Child Is Learning

Going to the library can become a habit that will enrich your child's knowledge and life. Regular library visits lead to regular reading. Your child will learn how to choose a few items from many options. Your child will learn how to behave in a library—being quiet and speaking in a whisper.

What the Research Says

Bilingual website Colorín Colorado offers great tips and advice on what to expect at a library. See "What to Expect When You Visit the Library," http://www.colorincolorado.org/article/what-expect-when-you-visit-library

Dear families:

When your child begins to recognize some letters in his or her name, this is often the very first sign of learning to read. First, your child sees his or her name as a "picture," next as a series of letters, and then he or she reads the letters together. You may find your child saying things such as, "My name has a *J* and so does yours," or "Look, Mommy, I see all the letters of my name on this page," as he or she points them out.

Engaging your child in letter- and word-finding games is a terrific way to support curiosity and literacy development. Pay attention to your child's interest in letters and words, and experiment using the words that are all around your home.

Sincerely,

Your child's teacher

NAME RECOGNITION

What I Need

Paper
Marker
Masking or painter's tape
Printed material, such as magazines, newspapers, or storybooks

What to Do

1. Help your child write his or her name on some paper. Decide appropriate places to hang the signs—perhaps on the bedroom door, near his or her toothbrush or hairbrush, or on your child's toy shelf or bin. Save one for a letter-finding game.

2. Play a game in which your child finds the letters of his or her name in storybooks, magazines, newspapers, or any written material. Sit together, and let your child explore the materials and point out the letters in his or her name as you browse the texts.

3. You can play this game when you are waiting at the doctor's or dentist's office, when you're sitting at an older child's soccer game, or anytime you have a few minutes.

What My Child Is Learning

Your child will begin recognizing the letters of his or her name and, later, will recognize his or her name by sight. Soon, your child will be able to read his or her name!

What the Research Says

According to researcher Janet Bloodgood, "As youngsters begin to explore written language, their name becomes a natural focus. Since the word young children encounter most meaningfully in print is their name, this is often the word they first attempt to write."

Dear families:

There are so many everyday things you have in your home that can serve as play and learning activity materials with your child. Old magazines are filled with colorful illustrations, photographs, and lots and lots of words.

There are many ways to engage your child with using magazines after you are done reading them. Start by finding words that start with the first letter of your child's name. If your child is engaged, you can continue to ask him or her to choose what to search for. For example, your child might like to look for items that are red or pictures of animals. Take note of the things he or she chooses, as they may well highlight some of your child's personal interests. Let your child browse through the magazines, and engage him or her in conversation about what you find together. Use vocabulary to describe images, or read words on the page.

Next, have your child cut out letters, words, and pictures and make a collage. Display the collage where the whole family can enjoy it.

Sincerely,

Your child's teacher

MAGAZINE SEARCH AND FIND

What I Need

Old magazines appropriate for children

Child-safe scissors

Large sheet of cardboard or paper

Crayons or markers

Glue or glue stick

Smock or old adult T-shirt

Old newspapers

What to Do

1. Collect magazines that your child can look at and cut up. Keep them in a special place so your child doesn't mistakenly destroy the magazines you aren't finished with yet.

2. Put old newspapers on the surface your child is working on. Have an old shirt or smock if you're concerned about the glue getting on your child's clothing.

3. Talk with your child about what the search will be: some or all the letters of his or her name or the family name, pictures of objects such as cars or food, pictures of items of a specific color, or let your child choose what to search for.

4. Encourage your child to cut out the letters or pictures. If he or she can't manage scissors yet, he or she can tear the photos out of the magazine.

5. Let your child make a collage on the large paper by gluing the photos on. The work can also be embellished by drawing with crayons or markers.

6. Talk about what he or she has collected and collaged. Label it on the page, writing the words your child chooses; for example, "My name is Alex, and I made a collage with all the letters in my name."

7. Display his or her work somewhere in your home and discuss the process.

8. Repeat a week or two later with a different collection goal.

What My Child Is Learning

Your child will begin grouping and categorizing pictures, letters, and words, which supports emerging literacy. He or she will develop fine-motor coordination by using the scissors.

What the Research Says

Researcher Lesley Morrow has found that literacy activities in the home and community influence a child's literacy development. A number of studies have documented the positive relationship between children's literacy experiences at home and the ease with which children transition to school.

Dear families:

Reading books with your child can be an everyday activity. It's a great way to snuggle with him or her and share a favorite storybook or discover a new one. As you read and explore the book together, your child will learn the fundamentals of reading and become acquainted with the language to describe different parts of a book. Drawing attention to the details of the book, the cover, the front page, the title, and so on will increase his or her understanding of how books work.

Teach your child the vocabulary for the parts of the book and let him or her handle the book. Your child's appreciation of books will grow with each opportunity to touch and feel a book and then read it together with a family member. Make storybooks a regular ritual in your family life, and your child will reap the benefits many times over.

Sincerely,

Your child's teacher

Gryphon House
www.gryphonhouse.com

BOOK KNOWLEDGE

What I Need

Storybook

What to Do

1. With your child, choose a book to read.

2. Settle down together side by side. Point to the title, and read it aloud. Point to the author's name and read that aloud, too.

3. Talk about the parts of the book: cover, title page, and body of the book, including illustrations or photographs. Think together how to hold the book and how to turn the pages so they won't tear. Talk about how to take care of books, such as not reading them where they might get wet. Talk about where your family stores books in your home.

4. Ask your child what the title tells him or her about the story. Listen as your child describes what the book might be about. Look at the author's name together, and talk about who wrote the story. There is usually a bit of information about the author at the back of the book.

5. If the book is illustrated, talk about the images as you read the story. Point out the difference between the illustrations and the text.

6. Begin reading. Show your child that, in English and in many other languages, we read books from left to right. If you come across a word your child does not know, try to figure out its meaning together. Often, you will have clues from the surrounding words (the context) or from the illustrations.

What My Child Is Learning

As you enjoy books together, your child will develop an understanding of how a book works. He or she will learn words to describe the various parts of the book, will learn how to hold and care for books, will learn to appreciate good stories, and will learn new vocabulary and a love of books.

What the Research Says

According to the University of California Ready to Succeed program, books are an excellent resource for children. They can introduce children to different people and places, expand their word vocabulary, stimulate their curiosity and imagination, and encourage their intellectual growth. Books also provide a means for special and enjoyable moments between adults and children.

Dear families:

Children are exposed to print art in many different ways, through the illustrations in their picture books, in museums, at school. They are seeing art in the world around them. To allow children to develop these aspects of their creative selves, we have a wide variety of materials at school that they can explore.

Drawing—using pencils, crayons, markers, and so on—is directly related to literacy development. As children become more skilled at controlling and manipulating drawing utensils, they are better able to try writing letters and made-up symbols. As their emerging literacy skills develop, they will attempt to create symbols—which, after all, is what letters are.

At home, the easiest and most basic materials you can give your child are crayons or washable markers and paper. If you leave these materials out for your child, you may find he or she will reach for them often without any urging from you. Together, find a special place to keep the materials where your child can reach them easily. Open-ended materials, rather than coloring books, offer your child opportunities to explore and grow in creativity, fine-motor skills, and emerging literacy skills.

Sincerely,

Your child's teacher

DRAWING

What I Need

Plain paper or a pad of unlined drawing paper
Crayons or washable magic makers

What to Do

1. With your child, create an accessible space to keep the paper and drawing materials.

2. Encourage your child to draw whatever he or she imagines. If your child needs encouragement, suggest drawing a picture of someplace you've just been or of a person or animal your child likes. Resist the urge to give your child a specific image to draw.

3. Give your child time to explore the materials. The picture might not look like anything you'll recognize. That's okay. Don't assume what it is; instead, just ask some questions, such as, "Do you want to tell me about your drawing?" "I see you've used blue. Tell me about the color choices you made." "How did you come up with this great idea?"

4. Listen as your child explains his or her thinking.

What My Child Is Learning

As your child explores what the materials can do, he or she will develop confidence and an appreciation of his or her own creativity. Your child will love having opportunities to express him- or herself while telling you the story of the drawing.

What the Research Says

Researchers Michelle Neumann and David Neumann have emphasized the value of simple, play-based activities to support emerging literacy skills. Sharing library books, scribbling and drawing, forming letters out of playdough or yarn, and singing rhyming songs are easy ways to support literacy learning.

Dear families:

Children's curiosity about letters is the beginning of emerging interest in literacy. You can support your child's interest about letters, words, and writing with simple activities at home.

One easy activity is writing on rice. You can set this up in minutes with things you have a home, and your child can use it over and over again. Your child will enjoy being able to write with his or her finger and then wipe it away by smoothing out the rice. This is a great activity for children who like getting things "right." They can correct themselves without having to cross out their work, and they can play as many times as they want.

Sincerely,

Your child's teacher

Gryphon House
www.gryphonhouse.com

WRITE ON RICE

What I Need

1–2 cups of uncooked rice
Ziplock bag
Serving tray or cookie sheet with four sides
Paper and pen

What to Do

1. Set the tray on a table, with a chair where your child can sit comfortably.

2. Cover the surface of the tray in a thin layer of uncooked rice.

3. Write out your child's name on a piece of paper. Ask your child to write the letters of his or her name in the rice with a finger.

4. Your child can try as many times as necessary. When done, he or she can smooth out the rice and start again.

5. Ask your child what other words he or she would like to spell in the rice. Write them out for your child on paper.

6. Let your child write other words as he or she imagines them to be spelled. Invented spelling is part of literacy development. Your child can write numbers and draw in the rice as well.

What My Child Is Learning

This is a great opportunity to practice letters and numbers without the permanency of writing with pencil and paper. Your child can gain confidence in his or her writing skills through this easy practice.

What the Research Says

According to researcher Roderick Barron, research indicates that seeing a word in print, imagining how it is spelled, and copying new words is an effective way of acquiring spellings.

Dear families:

Children have difficulty grasping a sense of time and knowing when significant events in their life will occur. It is conceptually hard for them to understand the passage of time when they don't yet have a clear understanding of days, weeks, and months or the language to express these concepts.

Creating a calendar especially for them can begin to bring these concepts from the abstract to the practical. Create a simple calendar on which your child can mark off the days until his or her birthday, when Grandma is visiting, or the next karate class. Post it on your refrigerator or family notice board at your child's eye level. If your child is impatient about when an activity is happening, refer to the calendar and count the days together.

This is an ongoing activity, and it may take many months of using a calendar before your child will truly grasp these concepts. Your child will be exposed to new words and will begin to gain a sense of control in his or her own schedule.

Sincerely,

Your child's teacher

CHILD'S MONTHLY CALENDAR

What I Need

Calendar
Markers
Stickers (optional)

What to Do

1. Show your child the calendar, and talk about it. Talk about the words for each month and day, explain how the grid of the week works, and talk about how each square has a number for each day.

2. Show your child today's date, and mark it in a special way. Say something like, "Today is the day we are starting your calendar." Consider letting your child put a sticker on that day.

3. Talk about what special events are coming up, such as birthdays, holidays, and family events, and mark them together. Decide with your child how to note them. He or she may want to draw small pictures to post for special days.

4. With your child, count the number of days until the next event. Encourage your child to mark an X on each day as it passes. Let this become part of your daily ritual together.

What My Child Is Learning

Your child is just beginning to develop an understanding of the sequence of time: later, before, after, today, tomorrow, yesterday. He or she is learning new words, such as the days of the week, but he or she doesn't yet understand what a week is. Your child is learning how a calendar works and how we track and conceptualize the passage of time. These concepts are very abstract, and each child's readiness to grasp them may vary.

What the Research Says

As authors Sallee Beneke, Michaelene Ostrosky, and Lilian Katz point out, young children are not developmentally ready to fully understand the concept of time. They can, however, understand terms such as later, before, and after.

Simply exposing children to calendars and talking with them about upcoming events in an engaging way—"One, two. Two more days 'til Grandpa gets here!"—is enough at this age.

4

Social-Emotional Skills

Dear families:

Your family is by far the most important social group in your child's life. First and foremost, your child finds love and security at home with family members. Each family has many different people making up its unique configuration. Your child will develop special relationships with all of these people.

Together with your child, create an album of pictures and photos of your family. This personal album will become a treasured book for your child because it's all about his or her family! You can add to this album over time to create a unique family heirloom.

Sincerely,

Your child's teacher

MAKING A FAMILY BOOK

What I Need

Loose-leaf binder or notebook
Loose-leaf paper
Glue stick or glue
Crayons, colored pencils, or markers
Family photos

What to Do

1. Discuss with your child who is in his or her family. Help your child name all the family members, and explain your child's relationship to them.

2. Suggest making an album to document all the members of the family. Label the front of the album with your child's name: for example, *Jessica's Family Album*.

3. Find or take photos of these family members. If you don't have a photo of a particular family member, your child can draw a picture of that person.

4. Help your child select which images to put in the album.

5. Create a page for each person's photo, and together with your child write that person's name and relationship. Leave an extra page empty if your child wants to draw a picture of that family member.

6. You and your child can work on this book over time, adding family as your child suggests.

> **TIP**
>
> If you're concerned about damaging fragile or special photos, consider making copies to use in the album.

> **TIP**
>
> To strengthen the pages, consider covering them with clear contact paper or plastic page protectors.

What My Child Is Learning

Your child will develop a special sense of his or her family unit—who the members are and how your child is related to them. He or she will have a special sense of belonging—this is my family!

Your child will develop sorting skills as he or she organizes the album and will learn vocabulary for the relations, word names, family names, and nicknames.

What the Research Says

Researcher Esra Dereli has found that the parent-child relationship is a significant factor for children's emotional understanding and emotion-regulation skills.

Dear families:

Children are incredibly curious about everyone around them, especially their own families. Each of us has an ancestry—where we come from, what holidays we celebrate, what foods we eat, what languages we speak. Teaching your child about your personal family history and rituals deepens his or her understanding of the world.

For your child, learning about your family is an important way to learn context for where you live and how your ancestors arrived there. A few cultural items will help you map out concretely where your family roots are. Think about the food, clothes, and holidays your family celebrates that are unique to your culture.

Helping your child understand his or her family culture and traditions will enrich him or her, help your child feel confident about him- or herself, and support your child in appreciating his or her friends who may have different traditions.

Sincerely,

Your child's teacher

LEARNING ABOUT OUR FAMILY TRADITIONS

What I Need

Objects that are unique to your culture, such as clothing
Paper and pen
Globe or map (can be online)

What to Do

1. Together with your child, find a few culturally unique objects. These could be articles of clothing, a photo of a family member in a particular item of clothing, or another object that represents your culture.

2. On a piece of paper, create a list with your child of foods that your family enjoys and that represent your culture. Talk about what makes a food special to your family. Do you prepare it for a holiday or is it part of your cultural upbringing? How is it different from what your child might eat at school or at a friend's home?

3. Look at the items you have collected, and talk about why they are special to your family tradition. When are they used? Who wears that clothing item and when?

4. Look at a map and point to a location of your family's origin. Talk about how many years ago your family moved to where you live now. If you have photos of these family members, now would be a great time to share them.

5. Take your time as it may be a lot of information, especially if your family is diverse.

What My Child Is Learning

Through understanding your family's roots and where the family comes from, your child will gain confidence in his or her uniqueness and learn to be considerate of others' uniqueness.

What the Research Says

A study conducted at Emory University by Robyn Fivush and others involved asking children questions such as whether they knew where their parents met and where their parents grew up and went to school. The authors found that the more children knew about their family history, the higher their self-esteem and the better able they were to deal with the effects of stress.

Dear families:

Learning about the world outside of home and school is important for expanding children's horizons. To gain appreciation of the arts and culture, consider taking your child to a local museum. Large cities often offer art and science museums. Many public institutions have free entries on certain days. But if you don't live in or near a large city, most communities have a museum dedicated to the local area, a famous local person, or a unique aspect of the local culture. In our area, we have the following museums:

_____

_____

_____

Taking your child out into the world to explore and have new experiences in museums will be very helpful in preparing him or her for kindergarten. This is a chance for you to support your child's awareness of the community and for your child to practice appropriate public behavior and to develop body-awareness boundaries. Ahead of time, talk with your child about behavior in public quiet spaces and staying near you in a crowd. This way, both you and your child will get the most out of your museum visit.

Enjoy the outing and special time together!

Sincerely,

Your child's teacher

MUSEUM VISIT

What I Need

Online access

What to Do

1. Besides learning about new topics, creatures, places, and art, in a museum children can also learn self-regulation and executive function. Search on the Internet for a list of local museums. (Your local library can help you with this.)

2. Decide what museum offers information and exhibits that will be most interesting to your child.

3. Prepare your child before you go—look at the museum website together, and talk about what you might see at the museum. Discuss rules of museums, such as speaking in a quiet voice, holding your hand or standing nearby, no running, and so on. Keep your visit to under an hour so it will be an enjoyable experience for all.

4. At the museum, quietly ask your child questions about what he or she sees in the various paintings, sculptures, or displays. Respond to your child's questions the best you can, and search for more information together at the exhibit.

5. When you get home, extend your child's learning by talking about what you saw. Give your child crayons, pencils, or paints and paper, and encourage him or her to interpret the art or exhibits however he or she is inspired to.

6. Talk about the museum visit several times during the coming weeks—you'll be surprised how different parts of the visit will reveal themselves in your child's memory.

What My Child Is Learning

Your child will develop an appreciation for culture, the creative process, and museums. He or she will begin to develop boundaries and an understanding of rules for visiting public places. Your child will build his or her sense of self, especially in a family with other children. He or she will learn new vocabulary.

What the Research Says

Introducing art, history, and science at a very young age contributes to the development of a child's identity and builds a foundation for learning in school and in everyday life. According to authors Kevin Crowley and Melanie Jacobs, young children make personal connections to what they see in museums, and they respond especially well when stories and the use of their imaginations are part of the experience.

Dear families:

As we prepare your child for kindergarten, we want to ensure that he or she will be comfortable with the new school. In our class we often discuss moving on to kindergarten and about how it will be the same as and different from our school.

While children are excited about kindergarten, they may be worried about little things: Where is the bathroom? Where will I eat lunch? How will I know where my classroom or the playground is? They may be anxious about who their friends will be.

To reassure your child and help him or her make a smooth transition to kindergarten, make an actual visit to the school building and, if possible, tour the school. Simply visiting the new building before your child begins attending will alleviate many concerns that your child might have about moving on. Try to arrange a visit this spring when you've chosen the school, and over the summer, anytime you pass by, point out the school to your child.

Sincerely,

Your child's teacher

VISITING THE NEW SCHOOL

What I Need

An appointment to visit your child's new school
Paper and crayons or markers

What to Do

1. After your appointment is set, talk with your child about where you are going and why.

2. Tour the school with your child, slowly giving him or her time to look around and ask questions. Make sure you visit a kindergarten classroom, the playground, the gym, the lunchroom, the principal's office, and even the bathroom. Take photos so you can view them later.

3. When you get home, ask your child whether he or she has any questions. Answer the questions as best you can. If you don't know an answer, try to find out and answer your child later.

4. Set out paper and crayons for your child, and discuss what you saw together. If you took photos, look at those with your child. Encourage your child to draw what he or she saw at the new school.

What My Child Is Learning

Visiting the new school will help alleviate anxiety your child has about going to a new place. Familiarity with the new place will build his or her self-confidence when the transition occurs.

What the Research Says

Researchers Sue Dockett and Bob Perry found that helping children understand what to expect from school is an important part of making a smooth transition.

Dear families:

There are many ways that children can develop a strong social-emotional connection to others. Through sharing with others, you can create an act of kindness and help your child develop empathy and consideration for other people.

This activity focuses on sharing our material goods with others and engaging your child in the process to help others in need. Perhaps your child has a cousin just a year younger than your child who could use your child's hand-me-downs. Or perhaps your child has seen a homeless person in your town. Could you bring that person food or a warm blanket? Is there a family who has just moved into the neighborhood who may appreciate a warm meal? With your child, think about how you can do an act of loving kindness through sharing.

Sincerely,

Your child's teacher

SHARING WITH OTHERS

What I Need

A conversation with your family about ways to share with others
Items to share

What to Do

1. Talk with your family about a need you or your child has noticed in your community. If you aren't sure about local needs, consider contacting a charity or church in your area. They are often great resources for identifying needs in the community.

2. Discuss ways that your family might help. Do you have clothing, toys, food, or books that your family might be ready to give away? Are there household items that could be shared with a new neighbor?

3. In particular, encourage your prekindergarten child to think of an item that he or she might give to someone in need. Keep in mind that this should be voluntary. Don't force your child to part with an item. Are there clothes that are too small for your child or toys that have been outgrown?

4. When you've gathered the items you want to share, take your child with you to deliver the items.

5. Afterward, discuss with your child how she feels. Share how you feel about helping someone in need.

What My Child Is Learning

Your child will begin to consider others in the world around her and start to share belongings. She will begin developing empathy and kindness toward other people.

What the Research Says

According to the Center on the Social and Emotional Foundations for Early Learning at Vanderbilt University, young children experience several stages of development that influence the development of empathy. Babies watch their families to learn how to react to other people's emotions. If parents and caregivers express loving, calm attention to their children and others, then babies learn that they are loved and how to show kindness to others. As very young children learn to understand their own feelings, they also learn to understand and care for the feelings of others.

Dear families:

Preparing for kindergarten includes several areas of readiness for "big kids'" school. One important area is self-help tasks. These include being able to dress themselves, put on their shoes, eat independently, and use the bathroom without assistance.

Although we work on many of these skills at school, it is helpful for your child when you also reinforce these self-help tasks at home. Encourage your child to do some self-help tasks for him- or herself, such as putting on his or her own coat. Let your child practice zipping the zipper or buttoning the buttons; don't assist unless you can see that he or she is becoming too frustrated. Ask your child to show you how he or she does it at school—you may be surprised at all your child can do!

Sincerely,

Your child's teacher

SELF-HELP TASKS

What I Need

No materials needed

What to Do

1. Observe your child in the following tasks:

    *   Eating: Can he or she eat independently? Can your child carry his or her plate to the sink?

    *   Dressing: Can your child dress him- or herself? Can he or she put on his or her shoes? Can your child put on his or her coat, mittens, hat, and so on?

    *   Personal hygiene: Is your child independent in the bathroom? Does your child wash his or her hands independently?

2. After observing your child, create a mental list of areas in which he or she needs assistance with these daily tasks.

3. Help your child become independent in these self-help areas. Be specific in giving instructions. Encourage your child when he or she is having difficulty, and praise your child's successes. Be patient!

What My Child Is Learning

Your child will begin to develop independence, confidence, and self-control.

What the Research Says

Researcher Janelle Montroy and colleagues have asserted that early behavioral self-regulation is an important predictor of the skills children need to be successful in school.

Dear families:

We want children to be safe and secure in school and in their neighborhoods.

When children are given the responsibility for knowing their personal contact information, they are empowered to take care of themselves. Children should have basic information memorized in the event of an emergency. They should know where emergency contact information is posted at home.

Although we don't normally support memorization as a teaching tool, personal information is one of the exceptions to that rule. While we review this information at school, your support of this effort at home is invaluable to ensure that your child knows his or her personal contact information. Together, we can ensure that your child will learn the necessary information and build important life skills.

Sincerely,

Your child's teacher

Gryphon House
www.gryphonhouse.com

LEARNING PERSONAL CONTACT INFORMATION

What I Need

Child's full name
Birthday
Street address, including the apartment or house number
Your name(s)
Your phone number

What to Do

1. Have a calm conversation with your child about the importance of knowing his or her personal information. Emphasize that your child is now old enough to know these things. Discuss a few scenarios when it might be important to know this information, such as should your child become lost in a store.

2. Ask your child what he or she knows already; for example, she is likely to know her first and last names. Ask for each piece of information so you understand what you need to help your child memorize.

3. Write out on a pad all the information your child needs to know, and read it together with him or her. Practice saying the information out loud. Remember to keep this fun!

4. Let your child practice dialing your phone number.

5. Show your child the places at home or in your car where you keep emergency contact information, such as a relative's or a doctor's phone number.

6. Point out the number of your home and the street sign where you live to help him or her make visual connections to learn the address.

7. If your child is having trouble remembering this information, make up a rhyme or a little song.

What My Child Is Learning

Your child will begin to develop a sense of autonomy and independence, security, and self-confidence.

What the Research Says

Lindsay Hutton, editor at FamilyEducation.com, says, "Life skills are essential for your child to learn how to be independent and become self-sufficient. Appropriate life skills will also help your child feel empowered, help develop his self-esteem, and aid in socialization and reasoning skills."

Dear families:

Children need to understand the wide variety of emotions that they will encounter on a daily basis and need to be able to respond to them appropriately. Being able to identify feelings and learning to handle them helps children feel good about themselves and helps them understand the feelings of other people.

Naming emotions and learning the cues for various emotions is essential for their social-emotional growth and ability to function well in society. This activity will focus on ways to recognize and learn emotional cues and will help build your child's coping skills.

Sincerely,

Your child's teacher

Gryphon House
www.gryphonhouse.com

RECOGNIZING EMOTIONS

What I Need

Magazines, photographs, and children's books
Cell phone, tablet, or computer (optional)

What to Do

1. Look through the magazines, photographs, and books with your child. Find images of people, and encourage your child to name the emotions he or she recognizes in the pictures. Model this by pointing to a photo and saying, "She is smiling. I think she is happy," or "Her mouth is turned down at the corners. I think she is angry or frustrated."

2. When your child identifies an emotion, ask, "How do you know?" Help your child identify the cues in the facial expressions.

3. Emojis are so popular in today's culture. If you have access to a cell phone, tablet, or computer, have fun looking at different emotion emojis and making those faces together.

What My Child Is Learning

Part of getting ready for kindergarten involves your child recognizing his or her own and others' feelings. This skill will help your child develop empathy for others.

What the Research Says

Child development experts and authors T. Berry Brazelton and Joshua Sparrow encourage parents and caregivers to provide children with structure, consistency, and realistic expectations for their behavior. This will help children gain more confidence in building friendships and joining into play with their peers. Social-emotional skills will stay with the child for life.

Dear families:

Preschoolers are just beginning to truly relate to other children and adults and to develop clear preferences about their social interactions with peers. They are learning to take turns, play together, and cooperate with others. They are developing emotional awareness of their own feelings and how they affect others' feelings.

You play an important role in nurturing your child's social and emotional development. You can offer support as your child navigates learning all these skills and can teach your child techniques to successfully incorporate acceptable behavior. Tuning into your child's unique temperament—and remembering that every child develops at his or her own pace—is as important as loving and nurturing your child.

Observe your child and encourage positive behavior with patience and love.

Sincerely,

Your child's teacher

Gryphon House
www.gryphonhouse.com

SELF-REGULATION AND CALMING TECHNIQUES

What I Need

No materials needed

What to Do

1. Spend time observing your child with other children, so you have a realistic understanding of your child's emotional behavior.

2. When you notice your child showing a strong emotion, name the emotion and how you know that your child has it. For example, "I see you're frowning. You look mad." This will help your child recognize and name emotions, an important skill.

3. If a tantrum or argument occurs and your child is visibly upset, sit with him or her away from the incident, and encourage your child to breathe in and out deeply until he or she is calm.

4. Talk with your child about why he or she is having a strong emotion. "Why are you feeling mad?" Listen to your child, then ask, "You're mad because Robert took your truck. What do you think you could do about that?" Help your child think of positive ways to make the situation better: "Do you think that telling Robert you would like your truck back would help? Could you try that?"

5. Give your child opportunities to make choices about how to handle situations in positive ways. Your child will appreciate having a sense of control and will gain confidence.

What My Child Is Learning

Children need practice in identifying emotions and interacting with others in positive ways. Helping your child learn how to calm down after an upset is key to helping him or her learn to manage strong emotions.

What the Research Says

Research by the Robert Wood Johnson Foundation shows that young children with more developed social-competence skills are more likely to live healthier, successful lives as adults—through the education and jobs they attain and in their overall quality of life.

CHAPTER 5

Math Explorations

Dear families:

Almost everyone loves fruit! An easy activity to do with your child is to prepare a fruit salad for dessert. Planning together, going shopping together for what's needed, and preparing the fruit salad is a terrific opportunity for your child to understand the steps needed to bring the fruit from the store to the table.

As you choose fruit in the market, talk with your child about what fruits he or she likes best and would like to put in the salad. Discuss where those fruits come from—read the label on the fruit to see what country it was grown in. Ask your child whether the fruit grows on trees or bushes. If you aren't sure, try to find out! Look at the unfamiliar fruits your market carries, and decide together whether you want to try one. Lots of new vocabulary words will come out of these conversations. And, your child will be engaged for the preparation stage at home.

I'm sure it will be delicious!

Sincerely,

Your child's teacher

FRUIT SALAD

What I Need

4–5 different fruits
Bowls
Cutting board
Safe blunt knife for your child
Juice squeezer (optional)
Aprons

What to Do

1. Plan a shopping trip with your child that includes buying the fruit needed for a fruit salad. Talk with your child at the market about what to select and where the fruit comes from. Decide together how many of each fruit you will need.

2. At home, wash the fruit together and prepare the work area. Talk about the reasons for washing the fruit: pesticide removal and cleanliness.

3. Start peeling and cutting fruit together, talking about what you are doing: "Look at this banana! It's a lovely yellow color. Mmm. How do you think it will taste?"

4. Your child might not be able to cut everything chosen. And he or she may want to taste the selections along the way—that's okay!

5. If you like, squeeze an orange or another citrus fruit over the fruit salad. Mix the flavors together. Yum!

What My Child Is Learning

When shopping, your child is learning to think about how much fruit is needed. As you are preparing together, you can talk about how many slices you are making and how many people you are feeding. All the motions needed in cutting and dicing will help your child develop his or her fine-motor skills.

What the Research Says

Researchers Lauren Finn and Maureen Vandermaas-Peeler found that parents can use cooking activities as an opportunity for teaching children about literacy as they use recipe cards and as a means of helping children practice basic math such as counting, measuring, and identifying shapes.

Dear families:

Children love to know how big or how small things are. They love to compare sizes, widths, and heights. You can help your child use actual measurement tools to accurately measure things around your home and to compare different objects and people. Encourage your child to notice the differences, and help him or her develop the language to describe these differences.

Measuring is an entertaining way to learn some basic math concepts. Be ready for some giggles in this play activity! Remember to follow these tips for a successful game of measuring:

- Start by measuring your child's height and then yours.
- Help your child choose things to successfully measure so he or she isn't frustrated.
- Encourage your child to choose large objects needing two people, and measure those together.
- Use appropriate language introducing new words to help focus your child on the process and result of the activity.

Have fun!

Sincerely,

Your child's teacher

Gryphon House
www.gryphonhouse.com

MEASURING THINGS AT HOME

What I Need

Measuring tape
Paper and pencil

What to Do

1. Show your child the markings on the measuring tape. Point out that these measure inches.

2. Show your child how to measure an object by putting the zero end of the measuring tape at one end of the object, then pulling the tape over the length of the object to the other end. Tell him or her that the number on the tape at the other end is the number of inches in the length, height, or width of the object.

3. Ask your child to stand against a wall in your home. Measure his or her height and mark it in pencil—you might make this a permanent spot where you measure your child over time. Talk about the number of inches in your child's measurement: "Wow! You're 40 inches tall!"

4. Lie down on the floor, and let your child measure you. Compare using language to distinguish differences: "I'm 60 inches tall. You're 40 inches tall. I'm taller than you. You're shorter than I am." (Note: At this point, don't worry about subtracting to find the difference. Just focus on comparing.)

5. Let your child measure different accessible objects around your home. Document the measurements on a piece of paper, which your child might illustrate later. If your child is able, have him or her write down the measurements. Otherwise, you can you do it.

6. Repeat this activity over several months. Ask questions such as, "Which one is shorter? How do you know?" You will be amazed at how much your child absorbs over time.

What My Child Is Learning

Your child is developing math concepts: measuring, comparing, and specific vocabulary such as *length*, *height*, *width*, *inch*, *tall*, *taller*, *short*, *shorter*, *wide*, *wider*, *long*, and *longer*.

What the Research Says

According to the National Association for the Education of Young Children (NAEYC) and the National Council of Teachers of Mathematics (NCTM), number and operations, geometry, and measurement play an especially significant role in building the foundation for mathematics learning.

Dear families:

Involving your child in everyday activities is a great way to support him or her in learning to count, sequence, and sort. Setting the table for a meal is an easy way to incorporate math learning and show your child how math is used in all sorts of ways.

As your child helps you, he or she will be helping you figure out what is needed for the meal on the dining table, how many people will be seated, how many of each item are needed—tasks that take a lot of concentration. Support your child in deciding what's needed and in organizing the table. Use all the proper words for each item, and help him or her learn where they need to be placed.

Your young one will love helping you and will feel good about him- or herself as he or she realizes how to participate in a daily activity. Over time, your child will be able to do it independently.

Sincerely,

Your child's teacher

SETTING THE TABLE

What I Need

Dishes
Utensils
Napkins
Place mats
Cups or glasses

What to Do

1. Think of some household tasks in which you can cooperatively engage your child. Consider, for example, setting the table, emptying the dishwasher, or sorting and folding the laundry. Let's say you've chosen setting the table. Ask your child to help you set the table for a meal, and gain his or her cooperation.

2. Count together how many people will be eating the meal: "How many people do we have? Let's see. There's you, me, Aunt Barbara, your brother, and your cousin Antwan. How many is that? One, two, three, four, five. Five people for dinner."

3. Ask how many plates, cups, utensils, place mats, and napkins you will need. Talk through this with your child. Together, collect the correct number of each item and set the table.

4. Narrate what you and your child are doing as you work together. "Let's put the place mats down first. Now let's put out the plates. Can you put a plate on top of each place mat?"

What My Child Is Learning

Your child will be learning one-to-one correspondence: the idea that, when counting objects, we count each object only once. With even the smallest task, your child will learn to work cooperatively, understanding the steps to accomplish the task and the need for attention to detail. Encourage your child to talk about what you are doing, and have conversations about not only the task but also why it is necessary. By learning to be a capable and helpful member of the family, your child will gain increased self-esteem.

What the Research Says

Researchers Douglas Clements and Julie Sarama assert, "Mathematical experience for very young children should build largely upon their play and natural relationships between learning and life in their daily activities, interests and questions."

Dear families:

Playing cards are an easy tool to use to play math-related games. At first, just share a deck of cards with your child and let him or her get acquainted with them. Point out the numbers, and see whether he or she can name any of them. (It's okay if your child can't yet!) Invite him or her to sort the card by suit. As your child does, talk about what he or she is doing: "I see that you put all of the heart cards in this pile. And you put all of these funny upside-down heart cards—they're called spades—in this pile." Invite your child to sort the cards by number. As he or she plays with the cards, your child will be developing number-recognition and sorting skills. This is math!

There are so many different ways to play with cards. You might have a favorite game that you can simplify for your child, or you could play Go Fish. Have fun together!

Sincerely,

Your child's teacher

Gryphon House
www.gryphonhouse.com

PLAYING-CARD MATH

What I Need

1 deck of playing cards

What to Do

1. Give your child a deck of cards, and let him or her play with them. See what your child does on his or her own while looking at them. Does your child automatically begin to sort them? If so, how?

2. After a few minutes, discuss with your child the names of the cards and the suits. Suggest ways to organize them, such as by suit, by number, by whether the card has a number or a face, or by color.

3. If your child is still interested, decide on a game to play together, such as Go Fish. Explain the rules, and show every step as you do a trial run of the game.

4. This is an activity you can have in your pocket at any time. It's a great way to keep your child occupied on a rainy day or when you are waiting for an appointment.

What My Child Is Learning

As your child explores the cards, he or she will be learning to recognize numbers and different suits according to patterns on the cards. If you play a simple game with your child, his or her attention span will increase as the child concentrates on what cards he or she needs.

What the Research Says

Card games can teach math and memory skills as well as strategic thinking, psychologists and sociologists say. The conversation and friendly rivalry that come with sitting down to play cards can strengthen family ties. Family games also can build children's confidence: The rules are the same for everyone, and it is fun to play a game in which anyone can win. In an article in the *Wall Street Journal*, William Doherty, professor of family social science at the University of Minnesota in St. Paul, says children can learn to win and lose gracefully, "to be happy but not gloat, and to lose and not pout."

Dear families:

Math learning is found everywhere! Even simple activities such as matching socks can support your child's ability to notice detail and compare characteristics. Sorting, too, is an important skill in both math and science learning. It requires that a child notice details, compare characteristics, and then decide how to organize a group of items. Sorting the laundry is a great way to practice this important thinking process. Turn your next laundry day into a meaningful learning experience.

Try the activity Simple Sorting as a way to support your child's learning. Remember the following tips to help your child get the most out of the activity:

- Preschoolers love to help and to feel useful. Encourage your child to offer ideas of how to sort the items. Listen to those ideas, and try them out.

- Encourage your child to notice details and compare characteristics. Talk aloud about the details you notice, and ask your child to do the same.

- Use descriptive language to talk with your child about what you're doing together. Count items together, talk about colors, describe textures, and so on.

Have fun!

Sincerely,

Your child's teacher

SIMPLE SORTING

What I Need

A pile of clean laundry

What to Do

1. Ask your preschooler to help you with sorting the clean laundry.

2. Put a large pile of clean laundry on a table or bed where you have plenty of room to work.

3. Invite your child to help you notice the types of clothes, bedding, towels, and so on in the pile: "Wow! We washed lots of socks this time!"

4. Ask your preschooler to give you an idea for sorting the laundry. "How can we tell whose socks are whose?" Listen to your child's idea and try it out. "Yes, we can make three piles: your little sister's socks, Mom's socks, and your socks."

5. Start sorting! As you work together, talk with your child about the characteristics of the items. "Your little sister's socks are tiny. They can go in this pile. Mom wears bigger socks. They can go this other pile. Your socks are in the middle—not tiny and not big. They can go in this third pile."

6. Enhance the learning by matching items within each pile. "Let's match your little sister's socks. This one has pink flowers on it. Can you find another sock with pink flowers? Yes! You found it. Let's put them together."

7. When you're done, your laundry will be sorted and ready to put away, and your child will be so excited to have helped you!

What My Child Is Learning

Preschoolers love to help and to feel useful. Your child will gain confidence with this fun activity. He or she will be developing math skills—noticing details, comparing characteristics, and then deciding how to organize groups of items. Your child will use descriptive words to talk about what you're doing together.

What the Research Says

Pattern recognition helps young children with later math and reading skills, according to researcher Julie Kidd and colleagues.

Dear families:

In our classroom, many activities include informal and formal explorations in mathematics. We want to encourage the children to engage in mathematical thinking in everyday activities. Numbers can be used to tell us how many, can describe order, and can measure and inform our world in countless ways.

As children learn to count, we want to ensure that they comprehend the meaning of the numbers and aren't just reciting a list of meaningless words. They are also learning to relate numbers to objects. One way that you can support this area of mathematical learning is by playing counting games at home with your child. Remember to keep it fun!

Sincerely,

Your child's teacher

SNACK-TIME COUNTING FUN

What I Need

Bite-size snacks, such as animal crackers or small cut-up pieces of fruit
Tray or plate

What to Do

1. Set five pieces of the snack on the tray or plate. Ask your child, "How many crackers (or pieces of fruit) are on the tray?" Listen as your child tells you how many, then ask, "How do you know?" Listen to your child's response. He or she may say something like, "I can see them." Or he may try to count the items, counting an item more than once or skipping over items. At this age, that's okay.

2. Say the following rhyme with your child, and use the snacks on the tray as you do.

   One, two, three, four, five little speckled frogs sat on a speckled log. (Point to each cracker on the tray.)

   Eating some most delicious bugs. Yum! Yum! (Rub your tummy.)

   One jumped in the pool where it was nice and cool. (Give your child one of the crackers to eat.)

   Then, there were four little speckled frogs. Glug! Glug!

   One, two, three, four little speckled frogs sat on a speckled log. (Point to each cracker on the tray.)

   Eating some most delicious bugs. Yum! Yum! (Rub your tummy.)

   One jumped in the pool where it was nice and cool. (Give your child a cracker to eat.)

   Then there were three speckled frogs. Glug! Glug!

3. Continue in this manner, pointing to the snacks on the tray, counting them, and eating them until they are all gone. Yum! Yum! Repeat as long as your child is interested, or until he or she is full. Your child will enjoy playing this game and reciting the rhyme with you. As he or she learns to count accurately to five, you can increase the number of snacks on the tray.

What My Child Is Learning

Pointing to each item as you count it will help your child develop understanding of one-to-one correspondence—the idea that we count each item only once.

What the Research Says

According to a joint statement by the NAEYC and the NCTM, young children have a natural interest in mathematics. Having fun math-related learning experiences helps children develop a positive attitude toward math.

Dear families:

Early experiences in sorting things into groups help young learners to better observe how things are alike and different—essential early literacy and math skills.

You have in your home a variety of materials that children can sort in different ways, and most preschoolers will do so with little encouragement. Take time this week to set up a button-sorting game for your child. You'll be surprised how many different ways he or she will think about sorting them.

Sincerely,

Your child's teacher

SORTING BUTTONS BY SIZE

What I Need

Collection of buttons in a variety of sizes, colors, and so on
Shallow bowls

What to Do

1. Provide the buttons and some bowls for your child. Ask him or her to sort the buttons, but don't tell your child how to sort them. See how he or she decides to sort them. Your child may choose to sort by size, color, texture, or some other feature.

2. When he or she is finished, comment on the sorting: "I see you put all of the blue buttons in this bowl and all of the brown buttons in that bowl. You sorted by color."

3. With your child, count the buttons in each bowl. Ask, "Which bowl has more buttons?" Ask, "How do you know?" Let your child explain how he or she knows.

4. Ask how else your child might sort the buttons. Encourage him or her to sort them by different attributes for as long as your child is interested.

What My Child Is Learning

Classification—noticing similarities and differences—and sorting are important skills in emergent literacy and math learning.

What the Research Says

Angela Harris of Michigan State University Extension says that matching and sorting, as with all other math activities, are best learned when they are part of a child's everyday life. Children need to see math being used in the real world. When they put a puzzle together, they are matching shapes. When they are putting on their shoes and socks, they are matching objects. While helping to clean up their toys or helping with laundry, children are sorting objects. Common activities that children experience during play and daily tasks provide many opportunities for them to learn math concepts.

Dear families:

Colors and shapes make up the world around us. A stop sign, a house, the wheels on a car, the shape of a doll—all of these items can be described using shapes and colors. Color and shape are ways children observe and categorize what they see. These very recognizable characteristics encourage children to define and organize the diverse world around them.

At school, we are learning to identify colors and shapes. There are several ways that you can support this effort at home in our activity this week.

Sincerely,

Your child's teacher

SHAPE WALK

What I Need

Cardboard or paper
Marker
Scissors (adult use only)

What to Do

1. Decide on a shape to search for in your shape walk. Draw that shape onto a piece of cardboard or paper, and cut it out. Give the shape to your child.

2. Ask your child to go on a shape walk with you around the house to find items that are the same shape as the cardboard shape. For example, if you decided to look for rectangles, look for household items that are rectangles, such as doors, cabinets, the refrigerator, and so on.

3. Take a shape walk around the neighborhood. This will help your child match the shape to objects in the environment and to notice same and different.

4. On another day, take a shape walk to look for another shape, such as a circle.

What My Child Is Learning

When your child explores different shapes in the environment, he or she is observing what is the same or different. This concept provides your child with a basic process that he or she will be able to use in observing, comparing, and discussing all that he or she sees and encounters.

What the Research Says

Researchers Mary Frances Hanline, Sande Milton, and Pamela Phelps assert that children learn about different shapes as they describe everyday objects in their environment.

Dear families:

Children love to count things and also love challenges. As your child is learning to count, one hands-on activity that you can use at home is a counting jar. Through estimating the number of items in the jar and then testing to see if the estimate is close to the actual number, your child will begin to develop *numeracy*—the understanding of numbers and how to work with them. This math game can be played throughout the year. Having a counting jar in a special place in your home can encourage a playful way to engage in guessing and counting.

Sincerely,

Your child's teacher

Gryphon House
www.gryphonhouse.com

COUNTING JAR

What I Need

Clear plastic jar with a tight lid
Small items, such as pennies or buttons
Sticky notes and pencil
Tray

What to Do

1. Place a small number—start with ten—of uniform items in the jar and close it.

2. Ask your child to guess how many items are inside the jar. Write that number on a sticky note.

3. Have your child empty the contents of the jar onto the tray, and then count the items together. Write the actual number of items next to the guessed number.

4. Talk with your child about how close he or she came to guessing the actual number. "Wow! You guessed six and there are ten pennies. You were so close!" Remember to keep it fun and positive! This is not a test.

5. Change the number of items in the jar (for example, take out two), and invite your child to guess again. Continue in this matter as long as your child is interested.

6. Later on, you can add more items to the jar and play again.

What My Child Is Learning

Your child will begin to develop the ability to count and to estimate quantity.

What the Research Says

Researcher Karen Fuson says that children need lots of experience with counting to learn which number comes next, how this number sequence is related to the objects in front of them, and how to keep track of which ones have been counted and which still need to be counted.

CHAPTER

Science Explorations

Dear families:

Every season presents opportunities for exploring the outdoors with your child. Going to the playground or running around the park are activities children may do every day. But opportunities to focus on the natural world right under our feet are waiting to be discovered.

Make a game of searching for insects and small creatures in your backyard, on your patio, and in the park. You and your child can learn a lot about the creatures that are right under our noses every day.

See what interesting insects and creatures you'll find!

Sincerely,

You child's teacher

Gryphon House
www.gryphonhouse.com

EXPLORING OUTDOORS: INSECTS AND CREATURES SEARCH

What I Need

Outdoor area
Magnifying glass (optional)
Small, clear plastic container
Camera (optional)

What to Do

1. Invite your child to come outside with you to search for insects and other creatures in your immediate surroundings. If you have a magnifying glass, bring it along.

2. Look carefully for insects. They may be hiding under a leaf or rock, in a crack in the sidewalk, on a tree trunk, next to a building, or near a water source.

3. When you and your child spot a creature, take the time to examine it. If your child has a magnifying glass, he or she can look closely at the insect. Remind your child to treat the creature gently.

4. If possible, gently place the insect in the plastic container, just to observe it for a while.

5. Talk about what it looks like: How many legs, wings, pincers, or antennae does it have? What colors does it show? What does your child notice about it?

6. If you have a camera, document the insect with a photo or two. Later, you and your child might search online for the insect and learn more about it.

7. At home, encourage your child to draw pictures of the creatures you found.

What My Child Is Learning

Your child will develop observation skills and begin learning to distinguish same and different features in the creatures you find. Your young one will be participating in *entomology*, which is the scientific study of insects.

What the Research Says

The National Research Council (NRC) says that acquiring firsthand experience through observing and/or handling small creatures helps children develop a healthy and curious attitude toward them, rather than one of fear or disgust.

Dear families:

Does your family travel to visit family members for the holidays? Do you travel for business? Do you have relatives who live in another state or country? Helping your child have some context for where these places are is important, as it will connect him or her to a world larger than the immediate, everyday neighborhood.

Using a map or a globe, consider marking off where family members live and where you or your child have traveled. If you travel for your work, your child will feel more comfortable being able to see where you are going. If your child misses a grandparent who lives far away, he or she will have at least an abstract understanding of how far that really is!

Keeping a map of where your family has traveled or where family members live is informative for everyone. Traveling will invariably lead to lots of stories about when you took that trip and what you did there or where you all slept at Grandma's house.

Sincerely,

Your child's teacher

WHERE IS THAT PLACE?

What I Need

Map of the world or the country you live in
Some map pins or small sticky notes or markers

What to Do

1. Show your child a map of your country or the world. You can find free maps through AAA or state or country tourism offices. You can also find them online. Check out http://kids. nationalgeographic.com/world/

2. Have a conversation with your child about what you will be tracking on the map. Are you marking where other family members live? Will you show your child where your family has traveled together? Will you show him or her where you have traveled?

3. Look at the map together. Point out where you live and mark it with a pin, sticky note, or marker. "This is where we live—Milwaukee. See? It starts with an *M. M-m-m Milwaukee.*"

4. Look for the place you've decided upon. "Abuela Martinez lives in Texas. Texas is way down here." Point to the spot on the map, and mark it with a pin or sticky note or marker.

5. Discuss the name of the place and the country it is in. Tell a story about that trip or ask your child what he or she remembers best from a visit there.

6. Talk about how long it takes to travel there and how to travel there: walking, riding or driving, or flying. Personal experience helps children understand maps. With a foundation from their own experiences, children will develop into successful map readers.

What My Child Is Learning

Your child will develop a sense of the world as a place larger than your community. He or she will begin to understand geography and that maps are tools to help us understand geography. Your child will begin understanding the concept of scale—maps reduce the size of an actual place.

What the Research Says

Blogger Jeanne Vergeront says that understanding place is an important way in which we make meaning of the world. We share places with others, return to places that hold meaning, and remember and tell stories brimming with place.

Dear families:

Every day you prepare meals for your family, and having a little helper in the kitchen can be a great way to engage your child in a learning activity. Children love to help cook—to measure, to pour, to mix, to taste, to watch as food cooks, and then to eat! No doubt, they'll eat what they prepared with gusto.

Children can learn so much from helping to prepare food—there's math in measuring out the ingredients, language development in new vocabulary words, and science in combining and cooking ingredients. Think of a dish your child enjoys that is easy to prepare with a young child.

You can first try a cold food preparation if you have concerns about the cooking aspect. Be prepared to make a bit of a mess—it's okay! As you prepare the food, talk about the process, and let your child add ingredients and mix.

Discuss what changes are happening in the ingredients. Most of all, enjoy sharing what you have prepared.

Sincerely,

Your child's teacher

COOKING TOGETHER

What I Need

Aprons
Step stool
Recipe
Ingredients for the recipe
Kitchen utensils

What to Do

1. Part of cooking with children is teaching them kitchen safety. Here are some basic safety rules to get you started: An adult should always supervise cooking. Always wash your hands before starting. Keep a safe distance from a hot stovetop or oven. Turn pot and pan handles toward the back of the stove to prevent accidents. Avoid sampling raw eggs or meat. Let your child practice cutting with a butter knife and graduate to a sharper blade only when you both feel comfortable.

2. With your child, choose the recipe you will prepare. Read the recipe aloud. Together, gather the ingredients and utensils needed.

3. As you work, let your child help you measure ingredients and combine them. Talk about how much or how many you need of each ingredient. Help your child use a measuring cup and measuring spoon. Talk about how the ingredients smell and taste.

4. Share your delicious creation with your family.

What My Child Is Learning

Your child will develop skills in the following areas: mathematics—measuring, one-to-one correspondence, numbers, and counting; language—vocabulary words associated with food preparation and cooking and the use of print; science—combining ingredients and changing them by cooking them; social-emotional—pride and confidence in his or her skills and abilities, independence, following directions, using thinking skills to problem solve; physical—chopping, squeezing, spreading, and mixing help develop fine-motor control and eye-hand coordination; and cognitive—curiosity, thinking, problem solving, predicting, and observing.

What the Research Says

Researchers Lauren Finn and Maureen Vandermaas-Peeler found that parents use cooking activities as an opportunity to teach children about literacy as they use recipe cards and as a means of helping children practice basic math such as counting, measuring, and identifying shapes.

Dear families:

Children have an innate curiosity about where things come from. Explore with your child the sources of some of the foods you and your family eat. As you shop at the grocery store, begin to think of ways to learn more about food. For example, wonder aloud, "Where do bananas come from? Do they grow on a vine?" "Mmm. I love carrots. I wonder: Do they grow on trees?" Ask your child to guess where some favorite foods might come from, then find out together! You can look online for more information on foods and their origins. For example, the National Public Radio (NPR) website offers links to maps of the sources of common foods. Check it out at http://www.npr.org/sections/thesalt/2016/06/13/481586649/a-map-of-where-your-food-originated-may-surprise-you

Your child's interest in food sources may extend to learning what you can plant in your own yard or on your own patio!

Sincerely,

Your child's teacher

WHERE DOES OUR FOOD COME FROM?

What I need

Internet access, either at home or at your local library

What to Do

1. As you shop for groceries or eat a meal together, engage your child in a discussion about the sources of some of your favorite foods. For example, ask, "Do you know where this apple grows?"

2. Ask your child to make a prediction about where apples might grow. Ask, "Why do you think that?" or "How do you know?" and listen to what your child has to say.

3. Then, find out! With your child, look online for the sources of some of your family's favorite foods.

4. When you learn the answer, talk with your child: "Were we right? Where do apples grow?" Then ask, "How do you think the apples get to our grocery store?" This will begin a whole new exploration!

What My Child Is Learning

As you explore the sources of foods, your child will begin to understand some of the processes food goes through to get from farm to table. Together, you will be learning new vocabulary and even some geography.

What the Research Says

In an article written by Janice D'Arcy and published online by the *Washington Post*, Andrea Northup, founder of the DC Farm to School Network, says that connecting children with their source of food makes them more apt to try those foods. She recommends planting and growing vegetables with children to help them make those connections.

Dear families:

Throughout the year, there are endless opportunities for planting and growing plants at home. You can grow houseplants and flowering plants in your home or on your balcony. If you have a yard, you can grow seedlings to plant in your flower or vegetable garden.

Children find growing plants fascinating. They are filled with wonder at the magic of something growing from a tiny seed. And they will enjoy taking responsibility for watering the plants. Growing vegetables encourages children to expand their healthy eating choices.

They'll love to see how plants begin to sprout and continue to grow each day. Figure out what kind of planting works for your family, and create a small garden, indoors or out!

Sincerely,

Your child's teacher

PLANTING AT HOME

What I Need

Flower or vegetable seeds
Potting soil
Any container with a hole in the bottom
Small shovel or old kitchen spoon

Watering can or pitcher
Chart or calendar
Paper and crayons

What to Do

1. Set up a work area either outside or indoors on a table covered with newspaper.

2. Ask your child to help you bring all the required items to the work area.

3. Decide together what seeds to plant.

4. Fill the container with the soil, and plant your seeds according to the instructions on the seed packet. Water the seeds.

5. Encourage your child to check the seedlings daily, and water only when the soil is almost dry.

6. Make a chart or use a calendar to record how long it takes for the plants to grow. Encourage your child to draw pictures of the plants as they emerge and grow.

7. If you're planting outdoors, when the seedlings have grown a few inches, transfer them into the ground.

8. Enjoy your vegetables, fruit, or flowers!

What My Child Is Learning

Your child will have hands-on experience with how things grow and will develop his or her observation skills. Your child will begin to understand that growing vegetables is a good idea—it encourages healthy eating. He or she will learn vocabulary: *grow*, *tall*, *seed*, *sprout*, *leaves*, plant names, and so on. Your child will develop gross- and fine-motor skills through physical activity.

What the Research Says

Researcher Dana Miller has found that when young children participate in gardening activities, they learn to communicate their knowledge about the world to others; to convey, process, and manage emotions; and to develop initiative, self-confidence, literacy, math, and science skills that will help them be more successful in school and better navigate the world.

Dear families:

One fun take on growing plants with your child is to use vegetables to grow plants. This is a simple way to start your home garden.

When you grow a plant from a vegetable in a clear jar, your child will be able to see the roots and sprouts as they come out. It's amazing to see how quickly these plants develop, and your child will be filled with awe watching the vegetable sprout.

Try it!

Sincerely,

Your child's teacher

GROWING PLANTS FROM PLANTS

What I Need

A clear glass or plastic jar
Toothpicks
A potato, sweet potato, root end of a celery bunch, or an avocado pit
Water
Paper and crayons

What to Do

1. With your child, hold the vegetable or pit upright, and insert four to six toothpicks into the middle section. Space the toothpicks so that when the vegetable or pit is set in the jar, it will be supported to hang in the jar rather than fall to the bottom.

2. Fill a jar with water almost to the top.

3. Set the vegetable or pit in the jar with one end in the water. The water should cover the lower half of the vegetable or pit.

4. Make sure the water is always covering the inserted section of the vegetable, and change the water once a week.

5. Check daily for growth. Encourage your child to draw pictures of the vegetable as it sprouts and grows.

What My Child Is Learning

Your child will observe growth and change as the leaves sprout and will connect to nature through this experience. Your child will learn new vocabulary such as *grow, sprout, seed, stem, root, leaf,* and so on.

What the Research Says

Researchers Vicki Bohling, Cindy Saarela, and Dana Miller have found that parents and caregivers can find dozens of nature-based experiences that promote rich learning and positive family interaction but cost little to no money.

Dear families:

Children are incredibly curious about how their bodies work and how they are the same and different from each other in size, shape, and color. It's important that children be comfortable with their bodies and feel free to move and play.

As part of our science studies, we use the correct anatomical names for all the different parts of the body. Consider visiting the public library for great children's books on the human body. You'd be surprised how excited four-year-olds can be to share the names they know and to learn new words for parts of the body beyond the basics.

You might learn a new body-part name, too!

Sincerely,

Your child's teacher

LEARNING BODY PARTS THROUGH SIMON SAYS

What I Need

Online access or another resource for body-part names

What to Do

1. Start by playing a simple game of Simon Says. In this game, a leader gives directions. The follower has to listen carefully and do the direction only if the leader says, "Simon says." For example:

    > LEADER: Put your hand on your head.
    > FOLLOWER: [doesn't move]
    > LEADER: Simon says, "Put your hand on your head."
    > FOLLOWER: [puts hand on head]

2. Your child may well remember this game from school. Catching someone off guard is fun, and so are lots of body-part names, so be prepared for lots of giggles!

3. Play this game together with the whole family.

4. As your child gains competence in knowledge of basic body parts, you can help develop his or her vocabulary by looking up names of other body parts; for example, instead of *head* say *cranium*, or instead of *shoulder blade* say *scapula*. Did you know that another name for *kneecap* is *patella*? That little groove over your upper lip beneath your nose is called a *philtrum*. Have fun learning new body-part words!

What My Child Is Learning

Your child will learn anatomically correct names for body parts and a sense of body awareness. He or she will develop memory skills, listening skills, and the ability to follow directions.

What the Research Says

Researchers Jocelyn Bonnes Bowne, Hirokazu Yoshikawa, and Catherine Snow have found that directly teaching young children new words in context increases the children's vocabulary.

Dear families:

Nothing is more exciting to children than seeing things change form and shape.

Water play is an experience that helps children learn science properties and have fun all at the same time.

There are many ways to play with water and ice at home. As you explore the similarities and differences of water and ice, ask your child to predict what will happen. Write down any questions and the answers you discover together. Review the results of your experiments. Your child will be thinking like a scientist!

Sincerely,

Your child's teacher

WATER AND ICE EXPERIMENTS

What I Need

Water
Ice tray or plastic containers
Freezer
Bowl or plate
Paper and pencil
Dishwashing gloves (optional)

What to Do

1. With your child, fill an ice tray or a couple of plastic containers with water. Place the containers in the freezer.

2. Ask your child to predict what will happen to the water. How will it change? How long will it take? Check back every half-hour to see how the water's properties are changing.

3. Note your child's questions and answers on paper.

4. When the water is completely frozen (this may be overnight), take the containers out of the freezer and look at the contents with your child. What does your child notice? How has the water changed? Write down any answers you now have to your child's earlier questions.

5. Handle the ice. What does your child notice? How is the ice different from the warmer water? (Note: If your child's hands get too cold, he or she can put on dishwashing gloves.)

What My Child Is Learning

You are exploring the scientific properties of water and ice and the stages of freezing. As you explore, your child will be learning new vocabulary, such as *freezing*, *thawing*, *melting*, *liquid*, *frozen*, *slippery*, and *cold*.

What the Research Says

Author Karen Worth points out that children are natural scientists. Their curiosity and need to make the world a more predictable place drives them to explore and draw conclusions and theories from their experiences. But, they need guidance and structure to turn their natural curiosity and activity into something more scientific. They need to practice science—to engage in rich scientific inquiry.

Fine and Gross Motor Skills

Dear families:

Making play materials with your child is a great way to be creative together. Playdough is one art material that can easily be cooked in your kitchen with ingredients you likely have on hand.

As it says on the website NAEYC for Families:

> Squishing, rolling, sculpting, molding . . . young children love to play with playdough. Add some props from around the home and playdough play becomes a powerful way to support your child's learning. This simple staple lets children use their imaginations and strengthen the small muscles in their fingers—the same muscles they will one day use to hold a pencil and write.

> Using playdough with you, a friend, or siblings supports your child's social skills such as sharing, taking turns, and enjoying being with other people. Playdough also encourages children's language and literacy, science, and math skills—all at the same time!

Try this terrific, long-lasting recipe at home. You'll see how a homemade play material will add hours of creative playtime for your child.

Sincerely,

Your child's teacher

MAKING PLAYDOUGH

What I need

2 cups flour
½ cup table salt
2 Tbsp. cream of tartar
2 Tbsp. vegetable oil

1 ½ cups boiling water
   (adult only)
Large bowl
Food coloring (optional)

Kitchen gloves (optional)
Newspaper
Aprons or old T-shirts
Plastic containers with lids

What to Do

1. If you plan on using food coloring, cover the counter with old newspapers to prevent the food coloring from staining. Put on aprons or old T-shirts to protect your clothing.

2. Ask your child to pour the flour into a bowl, then let him or her add the table salt and cream of tartar and mix to combine.

3. Ask your child to add the vegetable oil and combine.

4. Adult only: Pour in the boiling water. Be very careful—this will be hot!

5. Mix the ingredients until the dough forms, kneading as it cools down.

6. At this point, if you don't want to add any food coloring, you're finished!

7. Place each color of playdough in a separate plastic container, and store them in the refrigerator. They will keep for months.

> ### TIP
> Use food coloring gel for really vibrant colors. Separate the playdough into equal parts, and roll the parts into balls. Wear gloves to avoid staining your hands. Poke a finger into each ball, and put a few drops of food coloring into the space. Knead the dough to distribute the color evenly.

What My Child Is Learning

Your child will develop math skills by measuring ingredients, science skills as he or she observes how ingredients change when they are combined, and fine-motor skills as he or she mixes the ingredients together. Your child will learn new vocabulary such as *mix, measure, soft, lumpy, hot, smooth,* color names, and so on.

What the Research Says

In the article "Playdough Power," NAEYC recommends using playdough to support fine-motor, math, science, social-emotional, literacy, and language learning.

Dear families:

Once you have made your homemade playdough, it's time to play with it! Explore the playdough with your child, and see what he or she does with it. Your child might just want to make long, rolled strips or small balls and pile them up. Or your child might be interested in using some tools to work with the playdough. He or she might want to create something using twigs, straws, pebbles, or other items. Let your child explore!

Playdough feels nice in your hand and is very malleable. Ask your child how it feels in his or her hand, and search together for descriptive words such as *squishy* or *mushy*. Children can enjoy playing with playdough for a long time. Gauge your child's interest by his or her engagement. It's a great indoor or outdoor play-time activity and one that many children never tire of.

Sincerely,

Your child's teacher

Gryphon House
www.gryphonhouse.com

EXPLORING PLAYDOUGH

What I Need

Variety of household items, such as a fork, dull knife, cookie cutters, rolling pin, jar lids, and so on
Variety of materials, such as twigs, chenille stems, pebbles, leaves, straws, and so on
Newspaper or plastic tablecloth

What to Do

1. Make the playdough. (See the previous letter home for a recipe, or use a recipe you find online.)
2. Cover a table or counter with the newspaper or a plastic table cloth.
3. Collect items to use with the playdough, such as lids from jars, cookie cutters, a rolling pin, a dull knife, and so on. Set everything out in an area where your child can easily access them.
4. Encourage your child to explore the playdough. As he or she does, talk with your child about what he or she is doing.

What My Child Is Learning

Your child will develop fine-motor coordination, the cognitive skills of creativity and curiosity, and new vocabulary. He or she will learn to experiment and problem solve.

What the Research Says

As children explore and manipulate playdough, they are building strength in all the tiny hand muscles and tendons, making them ready for pencil and scissor control later on. Poking and pulling objects made from dough strengthens hand muscles and coordination.

Dear families:

Have you ever considered ways to include your child in your exercise routine? Children are able to follow most basic aerobic or yoga routines. Whether you are working out at home, in your backyard, or at a local park, bring your child along to work out together. You'll be surprised by how flexible and agile your child may be and by your little one's innate ability to follow your movements.

Make it fun! When you get children involved in exercise, you'll be teaching them a lifelong healthy habit!

Sincerely,

Your child's teacher

Gryphon House
www.gryphonhouse.com

EXERCISE TOGETHER

What I Need

Exercise equipment (optional)
Comfortable clothing

What to Do

1. Think of some easy exercises that you and your child can do together—perhaps yoga moves or stretches. Or consider going for a brisk walk.

2. Plan a time and place you can exercise together for no more than twelve to fifteen minutes.

3. Show your child the movement, and ask him or her to then try it with you watching. Gently guide your child if he or she needs help.

4. Make this a regular part of your routine. Over time, the two of you will develop a healthy habit of exercising together.

What My Child Is Learning

Your child will learn healthy life practices, body strengthening and awareness, and confidence and self-esteem.

What the Research Says

According to researcher Amika Singh and colleagues, physical activity and sports have a positive effect on children's physical health. Regular participation in physical activity in childhood is associated with decreased cardiovascular risk in youth and adulthood.

Dear families:

Working together on a puzzle is time well spent with your child. While he or she is dealing with the challenge of fitting the pieces in place, you have the opportunity to support and guide your child. There are so many different things your child is learning while making a puzzle. He or she is learning about shapes, improving eye-hand coordination, problem solving, and building fine-motor skills that will support him or her in developing handwriting abilities. Working on a puzzle is an easy project to do on a rainy day. Enjoy some together time with your child with this simple activity.

Sincerely,

Your child's teacher

Gryphon House
www.gryphonhouse.com

PUZZLES

What I Need

An age-appropriate puzzle with thirty to fifty pieces

What to Do

1. Find a quiet spot where you and your child can work on the puzzle. Set out the puzzle with all the pieces faceup.

2. Look at the picture on the box, and talk about the colors you notice and what might be some good areas to start with. Some people like to make the border first, so they look for corners and straight-edge pieces. Talk with your child about this strategy, and decide how you want to start.

3. Let your child use trial and error to fit pieces together. If he or she is getting frustrated, you may help your child, but encourage him or her to figure it out without your assistance.

4. After about fifteen minutes, ask your child whether he or she is ready to stop for today or wants to continue. Your child may take a few sittings to finish the puzzle or may do it all at once.

5. Leave the puzzle out for a couple of days after it is complete—your child may be interested in talking about the picture or the success of the process: "I did it myself!"

6. Put the puzzle away and perhaps have your child do it again in a month or so—especially if it was challenging the first time. This time it might be much easier.

What My Child Is Learning

Your child will develop fine-motor skills, which are fundamental for handwriting ability. He or she will begin to develop *spatial reasoning*: seeing shapes in context of each other to form a whole. When completing a puzzle, a child uses *mental rotation* to match up pieces of pictures. He or she will develop *eye-hand coordination*: When children flip, turn, and move pieces of the puzzle, they are learning the connection between their hands and their eyes. Your child will learn *problem solving*: figuring where pieces fit and where they don't.

What the Research Says

"Our findings show that spatial play (puzzles) specifically is related to children's spatial reasoning skills," says psychological scientist and researcher Jamie Jirout. "This is important because providing children with access to spatial play experiences could be a very easy way to boost spatial development."

Dear families:

Do you play music at home and occasionally break out into dancing while you are doing the dishes or cleaning the house? Your child is picking up cues for your musical taste and style every time he or she witnesses you enjoying music. So often we hear stories about how the early influences on musicians began with the music and styles they heard at home.

Dancing gets the heart rate up and makes you feel wonderful. Next time you're feeling the music, invite your child to dance with you and have a blast!

Sincerely,

Your child's teacher

Gryphon House
www.gryphonhouse.com

DANCING TOGETHER

What I Need

Music—any style that you love
Room to dance

What to Do

1. Choose some music with a good beat that you love.

2. Play it, and start dancing! Invite your child to join in.

3. Make a movement and encourage your child to copy you. Then let him or her dance a movement and you copy. Have fun!

What My Child Is Learning

According to the National Dance Education Organization:

- Dance involves a greater range of motion, coordination, strength, and endurance than most other physical activities.

- Dancing utilizes the entire body and is an excellent form of exercise for total body fitness.

- Dance fosters social encounter, interaction, and cooperation.

- Children learn to understand themselves in relation to others. Young children will create movement spontaneously when presented with movement ideas.

- Movement provides the connection between the idea and the outcome.

What the Research Says

Author and educator Rae Pica says that a competent mover will gladly keep moving, but a child who feels physically awkward and uncoordinated is going to avoid movement. So give children the time, space, and opportunity to move!

Dear families:

Time outdoors with the family isn't just for letting the kids run around while you relax. It can also be a great opportunity to actively reinforce what they're learning at preschool, extend their gross-motor play, and stimulate their brain development.

Challenge your child to hop on one foot, pretend to jump across a river, or walk backward. As your child plays, observe what he or she is doing, comment, and ask questions; for example, "I see you digging. Can you tell me about what you're doing?" Help your child notice details in the environment: "This tree bark is bumpy. Feel it?" "I hear a bird chirping. I wonder what kind it is." Remember to keep it fun and let your child direct the play.

Sincerely,

Your child's teacher

OUTDOORS TIME TOGETHER

What I Need

Outdoor places in your neighborhood

What to Do

1. Decide on a place to go where you and your child will have space to run around.

2. Engage in motion play with your child. You can lead, then your child can initiate a movement. For example, hop on one foot and challenge your child to do the same. Then, let your child do a movement that you copy.

3. Let your child choose a game that you can play together. Perhaps you could run a race or see who can walk backward the farthest. (Just be careful!)

4. Enjoy playing and moving with your child. You'll both benefit!

What My Child Is Learning

Your child will develop body awareness as he or she follows suggested movements, and he or she will get practice in following directions and listening. Your child will develop an appreciation of natural settings.

What the Research Says

Researcher Jeffrey Trawick-Smith points out that physical action promotes *sensory integration*, the ability to accurately interpret information being received by several different senses simultaneously. When children engage in physical play, their brains develop the ability to coordinate the different neurological regions responsible for sensory-based learning. When a child plays a racing game, for example, separate auditory and visual centers of the brain must interact to simultaneously interpret sound ("On your mark, get set, go!") and visual stimuli such as seeing others begin running and figuring out which direction to go.

Dear families:

Children need physical challenges and ways to develop their muscles and endurance every day. Spending time outdoors in the woods or at a local park is a great way for you and your family to enjoy being together and get some exercise. Go on a hike in the woods, and explore the natural sights with your child. Notice your child's endurance and motivation to complete the hike: "Wow! We walked up a big hill." Or, consider riding bikes together through your local park. Don't forget to take along some water so you can stay hydrated. Getting away from the home-school surroundings and being outside is refreshing for everyone.

Sincerely,

Your child's teacher

Gryphon House
www.gryphonhouse.com

TAKE A HIKE

What I Need

A local park or wooded area
Water
Snacks
Comfortable walking shoes

What to Do

1. Plan on a hike that will take no more than an hour.

2. Everyone should wear good walking shoes. Bring along bottled water and a snack.

3. As you hike together, take note of what's around you. Encourage your child to look up and look down to notice things in the environment. Talk about what you see.

4. Make this a child-directed experience. You may hike only 100 feet and then stop at a creek to splash your feet and throw rocks in the water before you continue on. Child-directed hiking is when the child leads. Let your child pick the pace, and try to look at things through your child's eyes.

What My Child Is Learning

Exercise will strengthen your child's body and help him or her learn what he or she is physically capable of. As you explore together, your child will develop an appreciation of nature.

What the Research Says

According to the *Head Start Early Learning Outcomes Framework*, early health habits lay the foundation for lifelong healthy living. Equally important, physical well-being, health, and motor development are foundational to young children's learning.

Dear families:

At school, we are working on writing our names. While they are learning letters and spelling their names in our class, children need a lot of practice learning to write. We've done a number of activities to prepare your child to learn to write his or her name, including making letters out of playdough, playing with letter-shape tiles, and labeling things with his or her name at school.

You can encourage your child to write his or her name at home. Most important is to make writing a pleasurable experience and not a chore. Help your child feel proud of his or her abilities and gain confidence in developing writing skills.

Sincerely,

Your child's teacher

LEARNING TO WRITE MY NAME

What I Need

Paper
Pencil, marker, crayon, or fingerpaint
Yarn (optional)

What to Do

1. Encourage your child to write his or her name on the materials you have provided, so you can see what skills your child has already mastered.

2. Starting from whatever point your child is at, write out his or her name in capital letters and ask your child to move his or her fingers over the letters to feel their shapes.

3. Ask your child write over your letters with a marker or crayon, tracing the shapes, or create dotted letters of your child's name for him or her to write over.

4. Encourage your child to "write" a letter to a family member and to write his or her name on it. Or your child can dictate a letter to you that you write down; then, your child can write his or her name at the end.

5. Providing opportunities to practice will help your child develop the ability to confidently write his or her name. Keep in mind, this may take many weeks and should be fun. Do not drill your child or use worksheets. Instead, use fancy markers, encourage him or her to shape the letters of her name in yarn pieces, or let your child paint his name with fingerpaints.

What My Child Is Learning

Learning to writing their name is often children's first step toward learning to write other words. Writing requires the fine-motor skill to hold a pencil and the ability to learn the direction to write and remember what the letters look like.

What the Research Says

Research confirms that reading and writing develop together as interactive and interrelated processes. Writing is an essential part of preschool literacy programs and supports children's development with regard to several components of literacy.

Dear families:

Four-year-olds have boundless energy and often need guided physical activities to release it. Finding ways to be playful and stimulating with your child while giving him or her direction and rules to follow can be challenging.

Help your child get some of that energy out by creating an obstacle course in your home—especially on a day when the weather limits outside play. Make a specific path for your child to follow in the largest room in your home. You and your child will have a lot of laughs and amusement from this activity.

Sincerely,

Your child's teacher

MAKE AN OBSTACLE COURSE

What I Need

Masking or painters' tape
Table
Jump rope or yarn
Chairs
Pillows

What to Do

1. Choose a large space in your home where you can easily move a few pieces of furniture to clear an area for the obstacle course.

2. Set up the room with several challenges, such as the following:

   • Tape a line on the floor for your child to walk on.

   • Set up a table for your child to crawl under.

   • Tie a jump rope or piece of yarn low to the ground between two chairs for your child to jump over.

   • Set out several pillows for your child to weave around like a slalom course.

3. Have your child start at the beginning of the course, telling him or her each obstacle as he or she progresses through the course. Make suggestions if your child is struggling, and compliment his or her abilities. Try the course with your child!

What My Child Is Learning

This activity will help your child follow a specific path with directions, concentrate, and listen to guidelines. He or she will learn what his or her body can do and will gain confidence in his or her abilities.

What the Research Says

Researcher Jeffrey Trawick-Smith says that the ability to coordinate different parts of the brain emerges rapidly in the early years for most children. It is easy to see how this connectivity of the brain—its ability to coordinate visual, auditory, tactile, and other stimuli, all at once—is crucial to learning.

REFERENCES AND RESOURCES

Barron, Roderick. 1980. "Visual and Phonological Strategies in Reading and Spelling." In *Cognitive Processes in Spelling*. New York: Academic.

Beneke, Sallee, Michaelene Ostrosky, and Lilian Katz. 2008. "Calendar Time for Young Children: Good Intentions Gone Awry." *Young Children* 63(3): 12–16.

Bloodgood, Janet. 1999. "What's in a Name? Children's Name Writing and Literacy Acquisition." *Reading Research Quarterly* 34(3): 342–367.

Bohling, Vicki, Cindy Saarela, and Dana Miller. 2012. *Supporting Parent Engagement in Children's Learning Outdoors: A Single Case Study.* Lincoln, NE: Dimensions Educational Research Foundation.

Bonnes Bowne, Jocelyn, Hirokazu Yoshikawa, and Catherine Snow. 2016. "Relationships of Teachers' Language and Explicit Vocabulary Instruction to Students' Vocabulary Growth in Kindergarten." *Reading Research Quarterly* 52(1): 7–29.

Brazelton, T. Berry, and Joshua Sparrow. 2006. *Touchpoints: Birth to Three: Your Child's Emotional and Behavioral Development.* 2nd ed. Boston, MA: Da Capo.

Carlton, Elizabeth. 2000. "Learning through Music: The Support of Brain Research." Child Care Exchange. https://www.childcareexchange.com/catalog/product/learning-through-music-the-support-of-brain-research/5013353/

Cherfas, Jeremy. 2016. "A Map of Where Your Food Originated May Surprise You." NPR, June 13. http://www.npr.org/sections/thesalt/2016/06/13/481586649/a-map-of-where-your-food-originated-may-surprise-you

Clements, Douglas H., and Julie Sarama, eds. 2003. *Engaging Young Children in Mathematics: Standards for Early Childhood Mathematics Education.* New York: Routledge.

Colorín Colorado. n.d. "What to Expect When You Visit the Library." Colorín Colorado. http://www.colorincolorado.org/article/what-expect-when-you-visit-library

Copeland, Kathleen, and Patricia Edwards. 1990. "Towards Understanding the Roles Parents Play in Supporting Young Children's Development in Writing." *Early Child Development and Care* 56: 11–17.

Crowley, Kevin, and Melanie Jacobs. 2002. "Building Islands of Expertise in Everyday Family Activity." In *Learning Conversations in Museums*. Mahwah, NJ: Lawrence Erlbaum.

D'Arcy, Janice. 2012. "Teaching Kids Where Food Comes From." *The Washington Post*, May 31. https://www.washingtonpost.com/blogs/on-parenting/post/teaching-kids-where-food-comes-from/2012/05/30/gJQAVy121U_blog.html?utm_term=.60aba2f9585b

Densmore, Anne. 2013. "12 Ways to Help a Child Make the Transition to Kindergarten." Harvard Health Blog, August 16. http://www.health.harvard.edu/blog/12-ways-to-help-a-child-make-the-transition-to-kindergarten-201308166611

Dereli, Esra. 2016. "Prediction of Emotional Understanding and Emotion Regulation Skills of 4–5 Age Group Children with Parent-Child Relations." *Journal of Education and Practice* 7(21): 42–54.

Dockett, Sue, and Bob Perry. 2003. "The Transition to School: What's Important?" *Educational Leadership* 60(7): 30–33.

Finn, Lauren, and Maureen Vandermaas-Peeler. 2013. "Young Children's Engagement and Learning Opportunities in a Cooking Activity with Parents and Older Siblings." *Early Childhood Research and Practice* 15(1). http://ecrp.uiuc.edu/v15n1/finn.html

Fivush, Robyn, Marshall Duke, and Jennifer Bohanek. 2010. "'Do You Know . . .' The Power of Family History in Adolescent Identity and Well-Being." *Journal of Family Life.* Retrieved from http://publichistorycommons.org/wp-content/uploads/2013/12/The-power-of-family-history-in-adolescent-identity.pdf

Fuson, Karen. 1988. *Children's Counting and Concepts of Number.* New York: Springer-Verlag.

Galuski, Tracy. n.d. "Ready or Not Kindergarten, Here We Come!" NAEYC for Families. https://families.naeyc.org/ready-or-not-kindergarten-here-we-come

Gross, Rebecca. 2014. "The Importance of Taking Children to Museums." Art Works blog. National Endowment for the Arts. https://www.arts.gov/art-works/2014/importance-taking-children-museums

Gunn, Barbara, Deborah Simmons, and Edward Kameenui. 1995. *Emergent Literacy: Synthesis of the Research* (Technical Report No. 19). Eugene, OR: University of Oregon, National Center to Improve the Tools of Educators.

Hachey, Alyse, and Deanna Butler. 2012. "Creatures in the Classroom: Including Insects and Small Animals in Your Preschool Gardening Curriculum." *Young Children* 67(2): 38–42.

Hanline, Mary Frances, Sande Milton, and Pamela Phelps. 2001. "Young Children's Block Construction Activities: Findings from 3 Years of Observation." *Journal of Early Intervention* 24(3): 224–237.

Harris, Angela. 2013. "Matching and Sorting Are Early Stages of Math Development." Michigan State University Extension, March 26. http://msue.anr.msu.edu/news/matching_and_sorting_are_early_stages_of_math_development

Harris, Justin, Roberta Golinkoff, and Kathy Hirsh-Pasek. 2011. "Lessons from the Crib for the Classroom: How Children Really Learn Vocabulary." In *Handbook of Early Literacy Research, Volume 3.* New York: Guilford.

Hiebert, Elfrieda. 1988 "The Role of Literacy Experiences in Early Childhood Programs." *The Elementary School Journal* 89(2): 161–171.

Hildebrand, V. L., and L. A. Bader. 1992. "An Exploratory Study of Parents' Involvement in Their Child's Emerging Literacy Skills." *Reading Improvement* 29(3): 163–170.

Hindman, Annemarie, Barbara Wasik, and Amber Erhart. 2012. "Shared Book Reading and Head Start Preschoolers' Vocabulary Learning: The Role of Book-Related Discussion and Curricular Connections." *Early Education and Development* 23(4): 451–474.

Hoff, Erika. 2006. "How Social Contexts Support and Shape Language Development." *Developmental Review* 26(1): 55–88.

Hutton, Lindsay. n.d. "I Did It All by Myself! An Age-by-Age Guide to Teaching Your Child Life Skills." Family Education. https://www.familyeducation.com/life/individuality/i-did-it-all-myself-age-age-guide-teaching-your-child-life-skills-0?slide=1

Jirout, Jamie, and Nora Newcombe. 2015. "Building Blocks for Developing Spatial Skills: Evidence from a Large, Representative U.S. Sample." *Psychological Science* 26(3): 302–310.

Joseph, Gail, et al. n.d *Presenters Scripts, Module 2: Social Emotional Teaching Strategies*. Nashville, TN: Center on the Social and Emotional Foundations for Early Learning, Vanderbilt University. http://csefel.vanderbilt.edu/modules/module2/script.pdf

Kidd, Julie, et al. 2013. "Effects of Patterning Instruction on the Academic Achievement of 1st-Grade Children." *Journal of Research in Childhood Education* 27(2): 224–238.

Kidd, Julie, et al. 2014. "Instructing First Grade Children on Patterning Improves Reading and Mathematics." *Early Education and Development* 25(1): 134–151.

Maguire, Jack. 1985. *Creative Storytelling: Choosing, Inventing, and Sharing Tales for Children*. Cambridge, MA: Yellow Moon.

Mason, Jana, and JoBeth Allen. 1986. "A Review of Emergent Literacy with Implications for Research and Practice in Reading." *Review of Research in Education* 13(1): 3–47.

Miller, Dana. 2007. "The Seeds of Learning: Young Children Develop Important Skills through Their Gardening Activities at a Midwestern Early Education Program." *Applied Environmental Education and Communication* 6(1): 49–66.

Montroy, Janelle, et al. 2014. "Social Skills and Problem Behaviors as Mediators of the Relationship between Behavioral Self-Regulation and Academic Achievement." *Early Childhood Research Quarterly* 29(3): 298–309.

Morrow, Lesley. 1990. "Preparing the Classroom Environment to Promote Literacy during Play." *Early Childhood Research Quarterly* 5(4): 537–554.

Munley, Mary Ellen. 2012. *Early Learning in Museums: A Review of Literature*. Washington, DC: Smithsonian Institution, Early Learning Collaborative Network and Smithsonian Early Enrichment Center. https://www.si.edu/Content/SEEC/docs/mem%20literature%20review%20early%20learning%20in%20museums%20final%204%2012%202012.pdf

National Association for the Education of Young Children and National Council of Teachers of Mathematics. 2010. *Early Childhood Mathematics: Promoting Good Beginnings.* Joint Position Statement of NAEYC and the NCTM.

NAEYC. n.d. "Playdough Power." NAEYC for Families. https://families.naeyc.org/learning-and-development/music-math-more/playdough-power

NAEYC. 2012. "Bond through Reading: An Interview with Mem Fox." NAEYC for Families. http://families.naeyc.org/learning-and-development/reading-writing/bond-through-reading-interview-mem-fox

NCTM. 1989. *Curriculum and Evaluation Standards for School Mathematics.* Reston, VA: National Council of Teachers of Mathematics.

National Dance Education Organization. n.d. "Standards for Dance in Early Childhood." National Dance Education Organization. http://www.ndeo.org/content.aspx?page_id=22&club_id=893257&module_id=55419

National Research Council. 1990. *Fulfilling the Promise: Biology Education in the Nation's Schools.* Washington, DC: The National Academies Press.

Neuman, Susan, and Tanya Wright. 2013. *All about Words: Increasing Vocabulary in the Common Core Classroom*, PreK–2. New York: Teachers College Press.

Neumann, Michelle, and David Neumann. 2009. "More than Just Storybooks: Promoting Emergent Literacy Skills in the Home." *Childhood Education* 85(4): 257–259.

Office of Head Start. 2015. *Head Start Early Learning Outcomes Framework: Ages Birth to Five.* Washington, DC: Administration for Children and Families, US Department of Health and Human Services. https://eclkc.ohs.acf.hhs.gov/hslc/hs/sr/approach/pdf/ohs-framework.pdf

Peck, Jackie. 1989. "Using Storytelling to Promote Language and Literacy Development." *The Reading Teacher* 43(2): 138–41.

Pica, Rae. 2008. "Why Motor Skills Matter." Beyond the Journal, *Young Children* on the Web. https://www.naeyc.org/files/yc/file/200807/BTJLearningLeapsBounds.pdf

Rittle-Johnson, Bethany, et al. 2016. "Early Math Trajectories: Low-Income Children's Mathematics Knowledge from Ages 4 to 11." *Child Development.* Published electronically December 6, 2016. doi:10.1111/cdev.12662.

Robert Wood Johnson Foundation. 2015. "How Children's Social Competence Impacts Their Well-Being in Adulthood: Findings from a 20-Year Study on the Outcomes of Children Screened in Kindergarten." Robert Wood Johnson Foundation. http://www.rwjf.org/en/library/research/2015/07/how-children-s-social-competence-impacts-their-well-being-in-adu.html

Schwerdtfeger, Julie, and Angela Chan. 2007. "Counting Collections." *Teaching Children Mathematics* 13(7): 356–361.

Shellenbarger, Sue. 2015. "How Family Card Games Teach Math, Memory and Self-Confidence." *The Wall Street Journal.* https://www.wsj.com/articles/benefits-of-a-family-card-game-1428444818

Singh, Amika, et al. 2012. "Physical Activity and Performance at School: A Systematic Review of the Literature Including a Methodological Quality Assessment." *Archives of Pediatrics and Adolescent Medicine* 166(1): 49–55.

Smith, Carl. 1989. "Emergent Literacy—An Environmental Concept." *The Reading Teacher* 42(7): 528.

Teale, William, and Elizabeth Sulzby. 1987. "Literacy Acquisition in Early Childhood: The Roles of Access and Mediation in Storybook Reading." In *The Future of Literacy in a Changing World.* New York: Pergamon Press.

Trawick-Smith, Jeffrey. 2014. *The Physical Play and Motor Development of Young Children: A Review of Literature and Implications for Practice.* Windham, CT: Center for Early Childhood Education, Eastern Connecticut State University.

University of California Cooperative Extension. n.d. "Selecting Books for Young Children." Ready to Succeed. http://ucanr.edu/sites/ReadytoSucceed/Books_for_Young_Children/

van Kleeck, Anne. 1990. "Emergent Literacy: Learning about Print before Learning to Read." *Topics in Language Disorders* 10(2): 25–45.

Vergeront, Jeanne. 2013. "Place Matters." Museum Notes (blog), July 31. http://museumnotes.blogspot.com/2013/07/place-matters.html

Worth, Karen. 2010. Science in *Early Childhood Classrooms: Content and Process.* Newton, MA: Center for Science Education, Education Development Center. http://ecrp.illinois.edu/beyond/seed/worth.html

INDEX

A

Animal crackers, 75

Aprons, 65, 89, 103

Art, 14–15, 36–37, 48–49

Autonomy, vi, 12–13, 18–19, 36–37, 54–57, 64–65, 68–69, 72–73, 88–89, 93–95, 106–107, 112–115

Avocado pits, 95

B

Balance, 3

Barron, Roderick, 39

Belonging, 44–47

Beneke, Sallee, 41

Binders, 45

Bloodgood, Janet, 31

Body awareness, 48–49, 96–97, 106–107, 110–115, 118–119

Bohling, Vicki, 95

Book awareness, 34–35

Books, 26–31, 34–35, 37, 59

Bowls, 65, 77, 99, 103

Bowne, Jocelyn Bonnes, 97

Brazelton, T. Berry, 59

Buttons, 77, 81

C

Calendars, 40–41, 93

Cameras, 85

Cardboard, 33, 79

Carlton, Elizabeth, 17

Celery, 95

Center on the Social and Emotional Foundations for Early Learning, 53

Chairs, 119

Charts, 93

Chenille stems, 105

Clements, Douglas, 69

Clothing, 107

Collages, 32–33

Colors, 72–73, 78–79

Comparing/contrasting, 66–67, 72–73, 76–77, 84–85

Computers, 59, 91, 97

Contact paper, 45

Cookie cutters, 105

Cookie sheets, 39

Cooperating, 12–13, 60–61, 64–65, 68–69, 72–73, 88–89, 108–109

Coping skills, 58–61

Counting, 3, 40–41, 64–65, 68–69, 74–75, 80–81, 88–89

Crayons, 33, 36–37, 45, 51, 93, 95, 117

Cream of tartar, 103

Creativity, 36–37, 48–49, 105

Critical thinking skills, 3

Crowley, Kevin, 15, 49

Cultural diversity, 14–17, 24–25, 34–35, 44–49, 86–87, 90–91

Cups, 69

Cutting boards, 65

D

D'Arcy, Janice, 91

Dancing, 110–111

Dereli, Esra, 44–45

Descriptive language, 12–13, 35, 72–73, 11, 104–105

Dishes, 69, 75, 99

Dockett, Sue, 51

Doherty, William, 71

Drawing, 36–37

E

Empathy, 52–53, 58–59

Entomology, 84–85

Environmental print, 2, 6, 8–11

Estimating, 80–81

Exercise equipment, 107

Exercise, 106–107, 110–115

Experimenting, 3, 98–99, 102–105

Eye-hand coordination, 88–89, 108–109, 116–117

F

Families

photo album, 44–45

storytelling, 24–27, 46–47, 86–87

working with, v, 2

Field trips, 14–15, 18–19, 28–29, 48–51, 64–65

File folders, 7

Fine-motor skills, vi, 3–4, 12–13, 32–33, 36–39, 64–65, 88–89, 92–93, 101–119

Fingerpaint, 117

Finn, Lauren, 65, 89

Fivush, Robyn, 47

Flour, 103

Flower seeds, 93

Following directions, 12–13, 88–89, 97, 112–113, 119

Food coloring, 103

Fox, Mem, 21

Freezers, 99

Fruits, 64–65, 75, 92–93

Fuson, Karen, 81

G

Gardening, 90–95

Geography, 46–47, 64–65, 86–87, 90–91

Geometry, 67, 78–79

Glasses, 69

Globes, 47, 86–87

Glue, 33, 45

Go Fish, 71

Gross-motor skills, vi, 3–4, 12–13, 92–93, 101–119

H

Hanline, Mary Frances, 79

Harris, Angela, 77

Head Start Early Learning Outcomes Framework, 115

Hutton, Lindsay, 57

I

I Spy, 10–11

Ice, 98–99

Ice trays, 99

Independence, vi, 12–13, 18–19, 36–37, 54–57, 64–65, 68–69, 72–73, 88–89, 93–95, 106–107, 112–115

Insects, 84–85

J

Jacobs, Melanie, 15, 49

Jars, 81, 85, 95, 105

Jirout, Jamie, 109

Juice squeezers, 65

Jump ropes, 119

K

Katz, Lilian, 41

Kidd, Julie, 73

Kindness, 52–53

Kitchen gloves, 99, 103

Kitchen safety, 89

Knives, 65

L

Labeling, 7

Language skills. See Oral language skills

Laundry, 72–73

Leaves, 105

Letter recognition, 2, 6–11, 30–33, 36–39, 87, 116–117

Listening comprehension, 7, 9–13, 97, 112–113, 119

Literacy skills, vi, 2, 8–9, 23–41, 65, 76–77, 92–93, 116–117

M

Magazines, 31–33, 59

Magnifying glasses, 85

Maguire, Jack, 25

Map pins, 87

Maps, 47, 86–87

Markers, 7, 31, 33, 36–37, 41, 51, 56, 79, 87, 117, 119

Masking tape, 7, 31, 119

Matching, 72–73, 76–77

Math skills, vi, 3, 40–41, 88–89, 92–93, 63–81, 102–103

Measuring tapes, 67

Measuring, 64–67, 88–89, 102–103

Memory skills, 16–17, 20–21, 56–57, 70–71, 96–97

Mental rotation, 108–109

Miller, Dana, 92–93, 95

Milton, Sande, 79

Montroy, Janelle, 55

Morrow, Lesley, 33

Music, 16–17, 110–111

N

Naming emotions, 2–3, 58–61

Napkins, 69

National Association for the Education of Young Children, 67, 75, 102–103

National Council of Teachers of Mathematics, 67, 75

National Dance Education Organization, 111

National Research Council, 85

Neumann, David, 37

Neumann, Michelle, 37

Newspapers, 31, 33, 103, 105

Northup, Andrea, 91

Notebooks, 45

Number words, 3

Numeracy, 38–39, 56–57, 64–65, 66–67, 70–71, 74–75, 80, 88–89

Nursery rhymes, 20–21

O

Oak tag, 7

Observation skills, 10–11, 14–15, 30–31, 84–85, 88–89, 94–95, 102–103

One-to-one correspondence, 68–69, 74–75, 88–89

Oral language skills, vi, 2, 5–21, 24–25, 88–89, 103

Ostrosky, Michaelene, 41

P

Page protectors, 45

Painter's tape, 7, 31, 119

Paper, 7, 31, 33, 36–37, 39, 45, 47, 51, 67, 79, 93, 95, 99, 117

Patterns, 70–71

Pebbles, 105

Peck, Jackie, 25

Pencils, 36–37, 81, 99, 117
        colored, 45

Pennies, 81

Pens, 39, 47, 67

Perry, Bob, 51

Personal boundaries, 48–49

Phelps, Pamela, 79

Phonemic awareness, 7, 9

Phones, 59

Photos, 45, 59

Pica, Rae, 111

Picture albums, 44–45

Pillows, 119

Pitchers, 93

Place mats, 69

Playdough, 102–105, 116
        recipe, 103

Playing cards, 70–71

Potatoes, 95

Predicting, 3, 20–21, 88–91

Print awareness, 6–9, 26–27, 30–35, 88–89

Problem solving, 3, 88–89, 104–105, 108–109

Puzzles, 108–109

R

Reasoning skills, 11, 57

Recipes, 89
        playdough, 103

Recorded music, 17, 111

Repetition, 20–21

Rhyming, 2, 20–21, 75

Rhythm, 16–17, 20–21

Rice, 39

Robert Wood Johnson Foundation, 61

Rolling pins, 105

S

Saarela, Cindy, 95

Salt, 103

Sarama, Julie, 69

Science properties, 98–99

Science skills, vi, 3, 48–49, 83–99, 102–103

Scissors, 7, 33, 79

Seasons, 84–85

Self-care, 54–57, 64–65, 114–115, 118–119

Self-regulation, 44–45, 54–61, 92–95, 106–109, 114–115, 118–119

Sensory integration, 112–113

Sensory play, 38–39, 102–105, 112–113

Sequencing, 40–41, 68–69, 81

Shapes, 3, 64–65, 77–79, 89, 98–99, 108–109

Sharing, 52–53

Shoes, 115

Shovels, 93

Simon Says, 97

Singh, Amika, 107

Singing, 2, 16–17, 20–21

Smocks, 33

Snacks, 75, 115

Snow, Catherine, 97

Social-emotional skills, vi, 2–3, 43–61, 103

Sorting, 3, 12–15, 32–33, 44–45, 68–73, 76–77

Sparrow, Joshua, 59

Spatial reasoning, 108–109

Spoons, 93

Step stools, 89

Stickers, 41

Sticky notes, 81, 87

Storytelling, 24–27, 34–35, 86–87

Straws, 105

Stress, 46–47, 50–51, 54–55

Sweet potatoes, 95

T

Tablecloths, 105

Tablets, 59

Taking turns, 2, 60–61

Time sense, 40–41

Toothpicks, 95

Transitions, 50–51

Trawick-Smith, Jeffrey, 113, 119

Trays, 39, 75, 81

Twigs, 105

U

University of California Ready to Succeed program, 35

Utensils, 69, 89, 105

V

Vandermaas-Peeler, Maureen, 65, 89

Vegetables, 92–95

    oil, 103

    seeds, 93

Vergeront, Jeanne, 19, 87

Vocabulary, vi, 2–3, 5–21, 25, 27, 32–35, 40–41, 44–45, 64–67, 88–97, 99, 103–105

W

Water, 95, 98–99, 103, 114–115

Water play, 98–99

Watering cans, 93

Websites

    Colorín Colorado, 19

    Family Education, 57

    National Geographic, 87

    National Public Radio, 90

Worth, Karen, 99

Writing skills, 2, 7, 30–31, 36–39, 38–39, 108–109, 116–117

Written symbols, 2, 6–9, 36–37

Y

Yarn, 117, 119

Yoshikawa, Hirokazu, 97

Z

Ziplock bags, 39

ML 10/19